I0475013

CHIEF
RESPONSIBILITY

Personal, Interpersonal and Organizational
Success Strategies

Dr. Paul Lockwood Brown

ISBN: 1456508768
ISBN-13: 9781456508760

Library of Congress Control Number: 2011900125

For my children:
Jacob, Rachel, & Paul Jr.
(J.J., Ray-Ray, & P.J.)

And for my true love, Harvest

Contents

Part III: Team and Organizational Success Strategies

Preface

Healthy human interactions form the foundation of our personal happiness and success. Characteristics of healthy human interactions include harmony, trust, freedom of speech and thought, truth, and loyalty. However, none of this can be achieved without each person first gaining greater self-understanding. It is only through increased self-awareness that we are able to reduce conflict and bring greater meaning to our daily interactions. Once the work of greater self-understanding begins we can turn our attention to gaining a greater understanding of our personal interactions.

I'm a lifelong learner. If you are like me, you're probably consistently observing the world around you, trying to make sense of it all. The need to become more observing became most evident to me upon enlisting in the United States Air Force. Everything I did in boot camp was uniquely strange and different from any experience I had had growing up in civilian life. As a young adult in boot camp, I wasn't observing and discerning; it was all I could do just to keep up with the physical, mental, and educational rigor of the experience. Upon graduation from boot camp, I finally realized that I had undergone a transformation.

The transformation was one from an undisciplined young adult to a United States airman. It started with the stripping of one's identity by shaving one's head and wearing nondescript olive-drab clothing for six weeks. The drill sergeants were well schooled in breaking down individuals and reforming them into disciplined young adults with all the ingrained characteristics, traits, and behaviors of United States airmen. When I returned home for the first time as a U.S. airman, everyone who knew me could clearly see the transformation. The physical transformation was obvious to me. What I was not aware of, however, was the way that I had changed my thinking and behavior. My family and friends were quick to point this out, and either lauded or chided me depending on their political orientation to the work of the United States Armed Forces. My boot camp experience changed me permanently; the U.S. Air Force had transformed me into a well-disciplined, observant, and principled person.

After serving five years in the air force, with three of those years stationed overseas in Europe, I was transformed once again. This time, it was due to experiencing the differences in norms, mores, and values of the many European countries I visited. There is nothing quite like the experience of traveling overseas to bring about an awareness of cultural differences and their effects on individual behaviors. As airmen, we were always briefed on cultural sensitivities and differences before traveling to a new country. It was during this time, when I needed to be highly observant to prevent unintended provocations due to potential cultural ignorance, that I became a student of observation. Yet even as I tried to maintain awareness of how my behaviors could impact others, at times, I acted in boorish, arrogant, and angry ways. I recall being denied service at a restaurant in Greece; upon realizing I was the victim of discrimination, I nearly panicked everyone in the place as I very vocally voiced my dissatisfaction and hollow threats of retribution. I was eventually escorted out and reminded never to return. Now, my goal was actually to get a meal; instead, I became the epitome of the Ugly American. As you will learn, being self-aware is only one step of the process. Disciplining oneself or trying to change personal behaviors is a very challenging part of personal growth.

Once I returned home and assimilated back into U.S. culture, I found myself deeply appreciative of gaining a better understanding of the uniqueness of each individual. With this heightened awareness, I was dumbfounded by my civilian life experience. Quite simply, it seemed to me as though virtually everyone around me was culturally ignorant. The ignorance I noticed was not intentional or by choice, but rather it seemed as though it was due to most people's lack of experiencing any significant cultural diversity.

My experience of people in the United States led me to believe that many U.S. citizens were much less aware than their European counterparts of how much choice and control they had over who they were and how they behaved. This lack of cultural awareness on their part puzzled me. I encountered people who were dogmatic in their ideologies and unwilling or unable to be open to dialogue about cultural differences. And while this was some twenty-plus years ago, to this day, my experiences with many are largely the same.

With this as a backdrop, my civilian life quickly became quite routine and predictable. I married and had a child. My wife and I bought a home. I started my career in management with a Fortune 500 company and spent much of the next decade or so climbing the corporate ladder, earning an MBA, and amassing material goods and wealth. It seemed as though I was successful at whatever I worked on. It wasn't long before I found myself in positions with increasing responsibility; I went from manager to director to CFO, finally landing in the corner office as a CEO. In the back of my mind during this process, though, was the nagging question of why some people were successful while others failed. The difference between success and failure didn't seem to be a factor of intelligence or hard work. To me, it seemed, the reason was more a function of self-awareness and self-discipline. In my desire to figure this out and apply some intelligent reasoning to my observations, I discovered the field of organization development (OD).

OD is the field of study that concerns itself with making positive planned changes in individuals, teams, and organizations through the use of two social sciences: psychology (the study of the individual) and sociology (the study of individuals in group behavior). At last, I had found a school of study that concerned itself with my passion in life. That is, the field of OD seeks to answer the questions of why some individuals, teams, and organizations are more successful than others. What are the differences? Are they individual differences? Is it about leadership? Is it just the luck of having a good team?

In search of these answers, I elected to enter into a doctorate program and begin my studies in OD. And, yet again, I had another transformational learning experience. I completed my thesis in record time, graduating first in my class. I also published my first book during that time and started my OD consulting practice and current teaching career as a professor of OD.

I have been consulting for over ten years now, and during this time, I have had the good fortune to work with many organizations. I have consulted with local governments, schools, the largest privately held company in the world, several Fortune 100 companies, nonprofits, small and large manufacturers, hospitals, law firms, and a host of other organizations. To my amazement, over the course of my schooling, management career, and tenure as a consultant, I found the more I studied the differences in people and organizations, the more I found them to be alike rather than dissimilar. It became increasingly clear to me that there were only two variables in every organization: how the people worked together and the inanimate objects they managed. The former is the focus of the book; the latter is left for others to discuss.

This book focuses on the three fundamental units of study in OD: the individual, the work of groups and teams, and the organization as a whole. All of the work is centered on improving and changing individual and group behaviors for greater benefit to the individuals, teams, and organizations. This book is divided into three sections, each containing three chapters corresponding to the respective OD unit of analysis. This book stands alone, with each chapter written like an individual short story in a collected work. Therefore, each chapter has a unique topic, so they can be read in any order. If you are concerned with organizational success strategies, you can read any of the three chapters in part 3 in any order. This is also true for part 1 (the study of the individual) and part 2 (the study of work groups and teams). *Chief Responsibility* is a must-read for those of you who know there must be something better out there with respect to your organization's culture or your interpersonal interactions. It begins with working on *you* as the main focus. While this may perhaps be one of the easiest books to read, the real work that you must do to help yourself continue on your journey of positively changing your life is most assuredly difficult. This is your *Chief Responsibility*.

The Man in the Glass

AUTHOR UNKNOWN

When you get what you want in your
struggles for self
And the world makes you king for a day,
Just go to a mirror and look at yourself
And see what that man has to say.
For it isn't your father or mother or wife
Whose judgment upon you must pass,
The fellow whose verdict counts most in your life
Is the one staring back from the glass.
Some people might think you're a
straight-shooting chum
And call you a wonderful guy.
But the man in the glass says you're only a bum
If you can't look him straight in the eye.
He's the fellow to please, never mind all the rest
For he's with you clear to the end
And you've passed your most dangerous test
If the guy in the glass is your friend.
You may fool the whole world down the
pathway of years
And get pats on the back as you pass
But your final reward will be heartache and tears
If you've cheated the man in the glass.

Part I:

❦

Self-Understanding — The Key to Greater Personal Success

Chapter One

SELF-AWARENESS AND SELF-DISCIPLINE —
YOUR CHIEF RESPONSIBILITY

What is your chief responsibility? At first glance, many of us will suggest that it is providing for our families, raising our children well, or being responsible and productive members of society. While these are all arguably true, I suggest that our chief responsibility is to foster greater self-understanding, to learn how our behaviors and interactions with others impact us and others, and to take responsibility for everything we think, say, and do. Without the self-discipline to hold ourselves personally accountable, we open the window for opportunities to place blame for our lives' circumstances on a host of uncontrollable variables. This leads to a victim mentality and learned helplessness. Regardless of our life circumstances, we need to recognize and take full responsibility for how we act and react to the joys and stressors each day brings. The bottom line is this: we have to hold ourselves accountable. We have to look into the mirror and take ultimate responsibility for each and every reaction we have and action we take. There are many ways of looking in the mirror. There are many qualified personality assessments, like the Myers-Briggs Type Indicator, DISC, FIRO-B, and the Creatrix Inventory. Personality assessments, while valid and reliable, are limited in their scope and thus are limited in their ability to address deep, personal self-understanding and the complexities of interpersonal relationships.

Taking Responsibility

America has become a nation of blamers. It is filled with people who prefer to absolve themselves of personal responsibility on virtually all levels. We want government to provide endless resources and programs for us instead of developing our own set of unique life skills. We want inexpensive or low-cost national health care instead of participating in reducing health care costs by exercising, eating right, and proactively managing our own health. We want head-start programs to parent for us during the early childhood years. We use the television as a babysitter rather than taking the time to have meaningful interactions with our children. We need to change our thinking and behaviors from looking outside for help in our personal lives to looking inward for the self-imposed limitations that prevent us from being more successful and having better personal relationships.

Change will not occur, however, until we decide whether we're going to look *out the window (for excuses)* or *into the mirror (taking personal responsibility)*. Looking out the window is easy; it requires very little effort on our part. We simply gaze out and adopt a victim mentality for the life we have been given and the choices we have made. When we look out the window, we passively accept the consequences that fate has given us, conveniently removing ourselves from the decision-making process.

Looking in the mirror is clearly the more difficult choice. It requires reflection, self-analysis, and an honest assessment of our behavior and the consequences of our actions. When we look in the mirror, we decide to become personally accountable, through vigorous self-questioning, for the outcomes in our lives. Looking in the mirror—that is, becoming more self-aware and holding ourselves accountable—is the only choice that leads to personal happiness. This is our chief responsibility.

There are, of course, external events in our lives that create unavoidable circumstances, but regardless of those powerful forces, we are still accountable for the choices we make and actions we take. I do not want to minimize the impact of major life stressors (e.g., the death of a parent, divorce, a major illness), but even in these situations—or perhaps more importantly *in* these situations—we need to be more self-aware and self-disciplined. Looking in the mirror and taking responsibility happens when we decide to say: "I refuse to be a victim."

Your Will: It's More Powerful than You Think

We all know the saying, "If it's going to be, it's up to me." But how many of us really practice it? Stop and think about it for a moment. The power of the will contains an infinite amount of energy. Roger Bannister willed himself to run a mile in under four minutes even after doctors declared it was physically impossible. Once he broke through that imaginary barrier, several dozen people repeated that "impossible" feat within the following twelve months. Was it physically impossible? No. It was a matter of will.

This is your wake-up call to understand the power of your will. While we cannot just simply will only positive experiences in our lives, we can, with a bit of introspection, tap into an inner power to help us bring greater joy to our lives by becoming aware of our behaviors, actions, and interactions with others. Let's take the example of being fired from your job. I was once terminated as an area manager for poorly interacting with and supervising the management teams of six restaurants. Now, of course, I didn't do this on purpose. I was blind to how demanding I was. I wasn't compassionate. I wasn't reasonable. The organizational performance came first at any cost. I was completely unaware of how my direct reports viewed me. In fact, I overheard one manager say, "I'll warm up to him someday like a snake warms up to a rabbit." Consider yourself fortunate if this has never happened to you. I had to realize that I was responsible for having been fired. When it happened, I was in shock; this was followed by anger and bewilderment. The bewilderment came when I realized that I hadn't even been aware the event was coming. How could that be? How could my performance or lack of skills get me terminated without my being able to see it coming?

I then realized that I was not even remotely aware of how my actions and interactions were affecting, not only me, but also my co-workers. It didn't take long for me to recall the immediate past and assess where I had made serious mistakes. I held up a mirror to my behaviors and realized that I had indeed made some bad decisions and acted poorly in some interactions. I was responsible for my being fired. Once I learned and accepted that it was I who had the problems, I was able to take corrective action and prevent these same behaviors from harming me in my next career move. I invite you to look into the mirror. It's not easy, especially when you've just been fired or severely chastised in your career. What I will assure you, however, is that if you simply choose to look into the mirror and begin to learn how to hold yourself personally accountable for all of your choices, you will not likely be terminated or disciplined without being fully aware of the reasons.

Let's begin the task of creating self-awareness by taking the reflection assessment. This assessment is essentially a mirror to certain aspects of our personalities. This ten-question self-assessment will reveal the degree to which you are holding yourself personally accountable. The reflection assessment was intentionally written using strong language, so please don't be disappointed if your score is low. *Always* and *never* are pretty strong absolutes, but that is exactly the point I am trying to make. Simply check the box that reflects your agreement with the statements made. Be brutally honest; nobody is keeping score but you.

ASSESSING MY ACCOUNTABILITY

Questions:		Yes	No
1.	I *always* take responsibility for my own actions; no excuses.		
2.	I always quickly admit my mistakes, apologize, and seek resolution.		
3.	I *never* blame internal or external environmental conditions for my decisions (the market, economy, ex-spouse, fatigue, etc.).		
4.	I take full responsibility for my physical health (that is, I'm not fat because I'm big boned or have a slow metabolism).		
5.	I like my lifestyle and if given the opportunity wouldn't change *any* material aspects (home, spouse, job, education level).		

6.	My sense of belonging is very high. I know where and how I fit into my world (family, civic life, spiritual life, work life).		
7.	I am *actively* working on changing unsatisfactory aspects of my life (dieting, counseling, exercising, etc.).		
8.	I eagerly awake grateful each day for the gift of the day and seek to positively impact myself and the world around me.		
9.	I *never* let my personal or family history limit my choices.		
10.	I live by the motto: "If it's going to be, it's up to me!"		

Scoring: Count the number of times you answered "yes" and determine your score.

Yes 8–10 times: Congratulations, my friend. You are uniquely in unison with yourself and your world. Do everyone a favor and pass this assessment along to someone you think will benefit from reading it.

Yes 4–7 times: Consider yourself average. It's time to take personal responsibility and live life to the fullest.

Yes 0–3 times: Count your blessings because this book was written for you. Good times are ahead if you read on.

I hope that now you have an idea of what areas of your life need work in terms of self-development. The assessment is simple and quick and provides a nice glimpse into personal accountability. If we slow the pace of our thinking and reflection and actually make fully conscious choices to guide our actions, we'll begin to lead more purposeful lives. Given that we only have one life to live; shouldn't we make choices actively rather than seeking fulfillment through fads, eating, clothes, television, sex, and all the other temporary gratifications in life? Select one opportunity area from the reflection assessment and begin to make yourself aware of your issues so you can start making conscious, purposeful, and positive decisions. Do not try to work on many items at once; it won't work. We simply don't have the mental capacity or discipline to modify multiple parts of ourselves at once. Remember to keep your focus and trust the strength of your will.

The only thing preventing us from becoming who or what we really want to be is ourselves. It is time to slay the dragons within. With the exception of a physical disability or clinically defined mental or emotional disability, we are born with virtually no limitations. All of our limitations are self-imposed or imposed by others until we are emancipated (that is, reach adulthood, at the age of eighteen in the United States). This can be illustrated with a few examples.

If we speak only one language, it is because we choose not to learn another. If we fail to educate ourselves beyond the required high school years, it is because we choose not to place a higher value on learning. If we understand only one religion, aren't we, by definition, limited in our experience with God? The divorce rate is so alarmingly high because we choose to swap mates rather than work through the difficult times. After all, who, in our disposable society, wants to fix a relationship that is broken when we can simply just choose to look for another life companion? Is it really in our best interest to continue this dysfunction without looking into the mirror and taking personal responsibility? We needn't limit ourselves. We must change the way we think about our lives, our actions, our choices, and, most important, our thoughts. Mentally slaying the dragons within is the first step to liberating ourselves from our own worst enemy—that is, our own nagging doubts and negative thoughts. Whether positive or negative, the power of our will cannot be understated.

Self-Discipline as an Art Form

Self-discipline is a rarity these days. It's time for each of us to stop looking out the window of irresponsibility by blaming others or outside forces for our problems. To turn from the window and look into the mirror of personal accountability, we must first realize the importance of self-discipline and take complete responsibility for each and every action we take. Change happens when we are willing to change the way we think.

Ask the experts why diets don't work, and they'll tell you that a diet is a temporary solution when what is needed to maintain a healthy weight is a lifestyle change. *Discipline* is a word that has negative connotations. Who among us wants to be disciplined? Discipline is normally associated with the parent-child relationship, in which parents discipline their children for various reasons. Many times, the child is acting out of ignorance. We often yell at children when they fail to look both ways before crossing a street, but when did we teach them about cars, traffic, rights-of-way, and crosswalks? Most often, we didn't. It was easier to just let them play and then yell at them whenever they encroached into areas of danger.

Either we are actively parenting and teaching our children well or we are letting them figure out proper boundaries on their own and then disciplining them. I learned this lesson early on with my first son. I had just come home from work and wanted to catch up on the news of the day. My son wanted some attention, but I was tired and wanted to relax and recharge my batteries, so to speak. He asked me if we could color together. I told him to color by himself in his bedroom and that I'd be in soon. He summoned me several times for various reasons, and I just told him to keep coloring. Finally, he came out of his room and said he was finished coloring and wanted me to see his work. When I walked into his bedroom, I was horrified to see that he had indeed made a wonderful drawing. The problem was the drawing was covering one wall of the room and not on a sheet of paper or a page of a coloring book.

What could I do? At once, I was angry with both him and myself. I was further conflicted by

wanting to praise him for obeying so well by leaving me alone and wanting to scold him or teach
him that we color on paper or in coloring books
and not on walls. I did the former and gave him
praise. I just couldn't find it in my heart to discipline him at that time. After all, I hadn't yet taught
him that we don't usually color on the walls of our
home. Further, I disappointed myself by being lazy
and not properly attending to the needs of my
child. This was a hard-learned lesson for me, and
it was then that I *began* to think and reflect on my
own lack of self-discipline and accountability for
creating the situation in the first place.

Self-discipline is an art form. Every two years,
through the Olympics, we celebrate the self-discipline of the world's greatest athletes. Similarly,
we celebrate the life stories of those who have
overcome daunting life circumstances. Do you recall the attitude of Christopher Reeve (he played
Superman in four films) when he was thrown from
a horse and paralyzed in 1995? From the initial in-
cident to his untimely death in 2004, his attitude
was a remarkable inspiration for us all. He didn't
lash out in anger. He didn't ask, "Why me?" He
didn't sue anyone claiming it was another's fault.
He kept his faith and will to recover and walk
again. His strength of character shone brightest in
his darkest hour. At first, his attitude seemed steely,
like Superman. It didn't seem real. We learned lat-
er that this was indeed his real attitude up until his
death. Not many of us face the adversities of life
like that. I know I don't. Yet that doesn't mean we

can't try to improve how we react to our lives and their many unforeseen circumstances.

Self-discipline is not limited to the mind. As a marathon runner, I work hard to keep my body in shape. I eat right and exercise regularly. My best time for completing the twenty-six-plus-mile race is just under four hours. Most of the races I've attended have been won by people of other nationalities, usually Kenyans. They run and win the race in about half the time it takes me to run the race. These runners are sprinting for the whole race. Remember the four-minute-mile barrier? These great marathoners are running twenty-six consecutive miles at about a five-minute-a-mile pace. I was astonished at their physical superiority. And yet their physical prowess is not supernatural. It is a function of the culture, the values, and the self-discipline of each individual.

Upon closer investigation, I learned that it was simply their lifestyle that enabled them to do this. They ate no fried or processed foods, ingested no alcohol, did not use tobacco, drank lots of water, and ate fruits and vegetables; they also had the self-discipline to run, run, and run every day. This is not a plea for vegetarianism or an invitation to train in sports. It is provided to illustrate the consequences of self-limiting and self-defeating behaviors—little by little, one day at a time. Often, it is not others who keep us from becoming who we want to be; we who do it to ourselves. We self-impose limits through our own self-doubt.

Taking responsibility for every action we take, regardless of the consequences, is what counts. It doesn't matter if we intended it or not; it happened. And when it happens, we need to own it. Owning our actions means standing up and taking full responsibility for them. We must do so without looking out the window to rationalize our behaviors. Further, this allows us to be human. To err is human, and when we err, large or small, it feels good to accept it, make restitution if necessary, apologize for our behaviors, accept ourselves as human, and move on.

You needn't master all of the tools, techniques, and insights proffered herein. In fact, by definition, by simply changing one aspect of your personal accountability, you are certain to embark on a new path of discovery and change.

In this chapter, we discussed the concept of absolving ourselves from our own thoughts and behaviors—that is, looking out the window to the many excuses we want to grab when things go wrong. Remember, the organization didn't fire me. It was my own lack of self-awareness that prevented me from being the best I could be for myself and the organization. If you've read this far, you've come to understand that it's time to look into the mirror and accept yourself for who you are. Further, you now know that you have far greater control over yourself than you ever believed possible. Finally, you now know that you can make healthier choices, which leads to a better life.

Chapter Two

WHY WOULD ANYONE WANT TO WORK WITH (YOU) ME?

Rarely, if ever, do we ask, "Why would anyone want to work with me?" Oh sure, we sell ourselves well during the interview process. We're nicely attired, prompt, well spoken, and sometimes quite nervous about our ability to convince others that we are indeed the right person for the job. This is much like our dating and courtship rituals. When couples begin dating, each person puts his or her best foot forward in hopes of creating interest and desire. If, however, a relationship follows, you can be certain that somewhere down the line, the courtship will end and the real relationship will begin. The real relationship includes all sorts of variables not revealed during the courtship period.

Eventually, our true selves are revealed. We find ourselves and others to be not as gracious, tolerant, or willing to serve others. We fall back into selfish patterns—not because we want to, but because it is who we really are. Facades tumble down. We experience conflict as a natural course of interaction and become ego defensive if our attitudes or actions are challenged. This does not make us bad people; this is just the simple reality. Maintaining quality relationships takes great effort, self-awareness, and self-discipline.

These same patterns also emerge at work. Our desires to please our bosses are replaced with feelings of complacency. Sometimes disdain and contempt follow if unrealistic workloads or deadlines are heaped upon us. But does it really have to be this way? Do we really have to switch jobs and partners so often as a remedy to struggling or failing relationships? Regrettably, yes, sometimes we do have to change the relationships because of circumstances beyond our control. But in most cases, there is a better alternative. The answer is as easy (and perhaps as difficult) as looking into the mirror.

Co-workers as Family

Do you realize that you spend more time with your co-workers than any other group of people in your life, including family? Let's take a look at the math. I'll start the process, and you can fill in the blanks and reach your own conclusion. There are 168 hours in a week.

Weekly Time Sheet:		
Time Allotment and Consumption:	# hrs	Description:
Total Hours in Week =	168	7 days x 24 hours (a)
Less:		
Sleeping hours =		= ____ x 7 nights (b)
Average work hours including travel time =		= ____ x 5 days p/wk (c)
Estimated hygiene time =		= ____ x 7 days p/wk (d)
Hours of television per week =		= ____ x 7 days p/wk (e)
Misc. (errands, shopping, chores, etc.) =		= ____ est. total p/wk (f)
Time with friends, dates, entertainment =		= ____ est. total p/wk (g)
Other (church, volunteering, etc.) =		= ____ est. total p/wk (h)
Total hours of consumption =		Sum rows (b) through (h)
Subtract total consumption from (a) =		Hours remaining for family

Don't focus on the accuracy of the time estimates; they obviously vary for each of us. Remember, we work five days and have two days off, not the other way around. The hours spent at the average workweek by far overwhelm any other category. Considering that many career people are working far more than fifty hours per week with drive time, the argument becomes even more compelling. Although not literally, the people at work are your *family*. These are the people with whom you spend most of your waking hours. And just like you didn't get to choose your siblings, parents, or even your crazy uncle in your real family, you don't get to choose your co-workers. My point is that developing positive workplace relationships is as important as developing any other relationship. The first step to this process is to look within.

Imagine if everyone in your organization decided to purposefully work on improving workplace relationships. Many people are under the misunderstanding that the people at work are just that: people at work; consequently, they end up treating them as objects rather than a person with real cares and concerns. Thus, they make no attempt to foster better relationships. As a result, frustration and stress build up. With increased levels of stress comes the need for coping mechanisms. These coping mechanisms take many forms from the simple (having a confidante) to the complex (cliques designed to defend departmental turfs and subvert enemy attacks from others within the organization). This is not the basis of good working relationships, nor is it an environment we want to spend most of our waking hours in, especially over the span of our careers.

Healthy work environments don't just occur. Occasionally, a team of people will blend together effortlessly and work in harmony, but this is not the norm. The reason teams experience dysfunction is because individual emotions, personalities, values, and beliefs, as well as a host of other factors, make up the sum total of who we are. And these aspects

of ourselves are presented every day in every interaction we have with others. Yet we never really get
the opportunity to look into any of these mirrors to
adjust ourselves accordingly and present our best
selves. Hence, workplace conflict ensues; everyone
on the team needs to learn to look into the mirror
and make adjustments for the good of the whole.

These mirrors of our personality and character do exist. We have personality mirrors, mirrors for
how we handle conflict, mirrors for our risk-taking
propensity, mirrors for our leadership style, and so
on. We don't often look into these mirrors for a
variety of reasons. Some of these reasons include
blind spots (what?), arrogance (who me?), and
delusions of grandeur (couldn't be!). Virtually all of
us need to look into these mirrors if we truly want
to get ahead and take charge of our lives and
our careers. No, you cannot ask your mother for
this feedback. That is what I call looking into the
fun-house mirror. Fun-house mirrors are the mirrors
that provide distorted images. These mirrors make
you look exceptionally thin or fat or somehow otherwise project a distorted image of who you are.
Sadly, the effort and self-discipline to look into the
mirror rests solely within.

The Feedback Fallacy

Do not ask your mother, friends, family, or
your direct reports (if you have any) for feedback;
they are not valid sources. Normally, these people would be happy to provide you feedback,

but it's usually not very accurate. The feedback is distorted because these people either want to make you feel good or want to avoid any unnecessary conflict. Mothers want their children to feel good about themselves. Direct reports want their bosses to like them because they have economic control over them (e.g., promotions, raises, etc.). Either way, the feedback does not accurately reflect your true self. What is required is an objective evaluation.

There are many ways to obtain an objective understanding of who you are. Psychological and behavioral assessments provide a mirror, as do 360° feedback assessments, through which people receive anonymous feedback from their bosses, peers, direct reports, and others. There are also many instruments designed to show us our conflict resolution skills our creative and risk-taking propensities, and many other characteristics. While many of these tools are very useful, they are limited by their inability to provide totally accurate reflections of our personality and character as a whole. The primary reason is that they fail to account for the subtleties embedded into our characters.

For example, two people who take a creativity assessment and get the same scores for creative ability may manifest their creativity in vastly different ways. One person's creativity may be aptly suited for a marketing campaign, while another's may be better suited to creatively solving manufacturing bottleneck issues. Yet, it is your whole person that your co-workers see. They cannot separate the different aspects of your personality from the whole. As a result, they form opinions about you as a whole person. These collective opinions serve as a basis for upward mobility on the positive side and pigeonholing on the negative.

An alternative method to obtaining accurate reflections of who you are is to honestly answer the following questions: Why would anyone want to work with me? Do I exhibit the traits and characteristics that others find desirable in a co-worker? Do I have enough self-understanding to know that I sometimes unintentionally hurt people by psychologically stepping on their toes, meaning no harm but nevertheless hurting them just the same? Gaining an understanding of this will help you to eliminate career-limiting behaviors and to earn the respect and success you deserve.

We all know getting promoted is a function of job performance, character, and commitment, as well as other variables that vary from organization to organization. Many times, individuals are left to discern what these tacit variables are. Few people are lucky enough to work for someone who champions their work, their goals, and their personal and career objectives. When we do find ourselves in this type of a relationship, we are quick to tout its worthiness. Unfortunately, if you are not in this type of relationship, you are left to figure out on your own how to become a person with whom others want to work—an attractive person. Gaining that attractiveness begins with an honest evaluation of yourself.

Taking the Reflection Assessment

To begin, you must first be willing to look at yourself in an objective fashion. A first step might be to take a quick glance in one mirror. Start by taking the Reflection Assessment, a simple self-assessment designed to assist you in discerning how attractive you are as a co-worker. This will help you to determine which areas are strengths and identify opportunities for improvement.

The Reflection Assessment			
Questions:		Yes	No
A.	I *consistently* ask for feedback in the following areas:		
1	Performance (productivity, results, etc.)		
2	Attitude (toward work, others, boss, reports, etc.)		
3	Self-understanding (knowing the impact I have on others)		
4	Opportunity areas (especially personal development)		
5	Commitment (to the organization's mission and others)		
B.	Would *all* those who work with me agree that:		
1	I am a sensitive and compassionate person?		
2	I receive feedback graciously and non-defensively?		
3	I show care and concern for the well-being of others?		
4	I value the work of every member and his/her contribution?		
5	I put the needs of others and the organization before my own?		

Scoring: Count the number of times you answered "yes" and determine your score.

Yes 8–10 times: Congratulations! Consider yourself fortunate for having a healthy sense of self as well as a very good sense of compassion for others.

Yes 4–7 times: Welcome to normalcy. By definition, most of us are in this category. Relax; read on. Welcome to the world of self-development for success.

Yes 0–3 times: Thanks for being honest. With a little effort and hard work, you'll be able to improve these scores toward a better you.

Personally, I really don't know if anyone wants to work with me. I have to ask. And I do ask because I care about myself and others. Demonstrating compassion is critical to your success. When we care for someone, we show him or her dignity and value. In my work as a consultant, I've come across many people who consistently tell me that they wish their bosses were more compassionate and empathetic. They don't necessarily want raises or promotions; they simply want their voices heard. They want to be respected. When workers feel included and valued, the quality and quantity of their work increases. As a by-product, they often receive recognition, bonuses, raises, and promotions. However, too many bosses are so concerned with accomplishing the mission or tasks at hand that they fail to realize that it is these other people who enable (or, conversely, hinder) their success. Many people in organizations are not fully engaged in their work, having resigned themselves to the fact that they are simply not valued for their input.

The opposite of compassion is indifference. To be indifferent to someone is the ultimate selfishness. Showing indifference to a person undermines positive working relationships, yet many bosses show indifference toward their team members every day. Some do this intentionally, while others do so from a lack of awareness. Either way, acting indifferently towards co-workers shows a lack of respect and dignity for the other person, as well as poor self-understanding. I think we'd all agree, intuitively speaking, that we don't like to work with selfish people. To tell an executive, a manager, or your boss that he or she doesn't care is both a difficult task and generally not your role as a subordinate.

Your job is to do your work well and work on yourself. Do not work on, worry about, or try to help others. People must be respected for where they are in terms of their own self-development—yes, even those who are selfish, ignorant, or otherwise predisposed to seemingly eternal complacency. While it may be tempting to offer this book to that special someone you find truly irritating, doing so would signal that you still have your own work to do. Work on yourself, and you'll be surprised at how others begin to treat you. A surefire way to get others to treat you differently is to begin to behave differently yourself. This can be simply illustrated with the use of a smile. Smile and greet a co-worker, and the likelihood of a return smile and greeting is very high. Similarly, ignoring a co-worker will yield the same: no interaction.

So smiles beget smiles and not interacting begets the same. How quick are you to smile and offer a word of warm welcome?

Working on Yourself to Help Your Relationships

All relationships involve at least two people. If you want to break a negative behavioral pattern, begin to behave differently yourself; others will have no choice but to react differently themselves. For example, let's say there is a co-worker who knows you have a pet peeve. Sometimes, for reasons unknown, they may choose to act in a way that they know will trigger your pet peeve. When this occurs, you probably react in anger or harbor resentment. In order to break this cycle, it is up to you to change the way you react. At this point, we ought to be able to realize that since we can't change anyone else, it behooves us to change the way we behave (in this case our reaction). If the stimulus doesn't trigger the same reaction in us—that is, provoke the intended response—the offensive behavior will stop because it no longer has the desired effect.

Remember, the idea here is to work on yourself. Trying to work toward changing another person's behavior or attitude is an exercise in futility. Focus on making yourself more attractive as both an individual and a team member. Be careful to not overtly focus on yourself. Nothing is worse than a braggart boasting about him/herself and his/her accomplishments. This behavior is obvious to others, seems selfish, and has a tendency to cause resentment. The idea is to quietly learn how to identify the person you want to become and work toward this. We all have aspirations and dreams. The question becomes: what are we going to do to make them become reality?

Visualizing Success

The mantra may sound a little silly, but it's true: "Be what you want to become and you will become what you want to be." Many great athletes speak about visualization. They visualize themselves winning the race, scoring the goal, or being the star. They picture themselves over and over again as a winner. They focus not on what they want but rather on what they know to be true: deep down inside, they know they are winners. They know who they are, and they know who they want to be. Many of the world's greatest athletes, as well as the greatest people in all pursuits of life, have one trait in common: *humility*. This is not a forced humility, but a genuine feeling of being blessed with a special talent, purpose, or passion for some aspect of life. While they acknowledge their greatness, they remain forever in touch with their inner selves. They adopt an attitude that says, simply, "I'm just being me. I love life. I love what I'm doing. I'm blessed." They have great role awareness. They know when it is their turn to lead, follow, or get out of the way. This is the beginning of good leadership: good self-understanding.

I often ask people what their leadership or management style is. Many times, people respond with a slate of lofty platitudes, like having an open-door policy, giving people the freedom they need to work, or focusing on results. Unfortunately, regardless of what they say, it inevitably boils down into a style of leadership that they themselves prefer. That is, if they allow others many degrees of freedom, it is often because they, themselves, want a large degree of freedom to do their own jobs well and with greater satisfaction.

An excellent leadership style is one in which the boss asks each individual how he or she would like to be led. Direct reports won't speak up for themselves; they have to be asked about their preferences in order to best serve their interests. For example, some people like to start their week out by visiting and catching up with others on the weekend's events. Others like to begin their day by checking calendars, e-mails, and agendas for the upcoming week. Others don't want to be spoken to until they've had their first cup of coffee. In each case, a good leader will allow a little time for each individual to begin the workweek in his or her own way. Failing to allow this only produces frustration from the onset of the workweek. A good leader knows that in order to lead people, he or she must have followers. This leadership style is designed to meet the individual needs of each person on the team. It is far better than adopting a leadership style that serves the personal needs of the leader and ignores the wishes of the people who work for him or her. These behaviors are not limited to the leaders of an organization. We all need to become aware of this concept and begin applying it.

Putting to rest the question of why anyone would want to work with you is not an easy task. It requires you to hold up a mirror and be okay with what is reflected back. It requires honoring, respecting, and accepting each person (including yourself) in terms of self-development. It requires the self-discipline to control your assumptions, to learn how to say, "I'm sorry," and to focus your attention on yourself rather than on others. It involves self-inflicted tough love. Further, it requires making conscious choices about how you want to live a meaningful life.

A "meaningful life" has a different definition for each of us, and defining what it is for you is an important task. A meaningful life for a priest attending to his parish is different from that of a scientist looking for a cure for cancer or a mother or father parenting well to develop well-adjusted, healthy adults. Regardless of our chosen professions or lines of work, we can all live more meaningful lives. It simply means we choose to develop greater self-understanding and learn how to develop healthier interpersonal relationships on all levels, from family to co-workers to all others with whom we interact.

Once again, this is not an easy path. Making strides toward gaining control over yourself, your life choices, and your career is difficult, but rewarding. However, the rewards for accomplishing that which is most challenging to us are disproportionately large. They are exponential in nature. They come coupled with true joy, happiness, and success. They are ours for the taking, if we accept the challenge to look within, focus on, and begin working on ourselves. They allow us to become who we really are, enabling us to take off the many masks we wear to cope with the challenges of the day. This permits us to begin to lead more meaningful lives. It all starts with learning about what it means to live a principled life. We explore this concept in detail in the next chapter.

Chapter Three

LIVING A PRINCIPLED LIFE—TAKING OFF THE MASKS THAT HIDE OUR TRUE SELVES

We all wear masks to a certain degree. Some of us live such masked lives that we claim others don't know or understand who we really are. Wearing different masks isn't necessarily bad. A mask is an attitude we don in situations in which we don't feel like we can just be ourselves. I don the mask of piety whenever I'm in the presence of the clergy. I'm quite certain that it's transparent, but it nevertheless keeps me from inadvertently swearing and causing an embarrassing moment. I similarly don a mask of demureness when stopped by a police officer. We need to first understand that donning masks in our everyday lives is simply a metaphor for hiding parts of our personality that we don't want others to see. These masks are usually transparent to others, inhibit true dialogue, and require a great deal of energy to maintain.

Wearing Masks—Hiding Our True Selves

So why do we choose to wear these masks? The reasons are many and varied. Mostly, it is an attempt to protect ourselves and our egos. When I don a mask, I am saying to myself that I can't be who I really am in this situation. I adopt an attitude of behaving in ways that I think are expected of me rather than just being myself. In these situations, I have to anticipate how another wants me to behave or react. This can be exhausting work. This, in turn, leads me to curtail the way I say things. And that leads me to say one thing to your face and quite another to your back. This, of course, ultimately leads to passive-aggressive behavior, and there is nothing genuine or loving in behaving this way.

For example, have you ever agreed with someone just to end a conversation? Have you ever pretended to agree with another person's advice? You might thank someone for giving you advice with no implication that you intend to follow the advice. Can you sense when people are being disingenuous? Do you realize that they, too, can sense it when you are being disingenuous? All of these are examples of wearing masks in our interactions with others. The masks we wear distort our relationships. Learning how to remove them and realizing the benefits of authentic dialogue is the goal of this chapter.

Removing Our Masks

In order to take the masks off, we first must confess to ourselves that we do indeed wear masks. This is an act of courage. It means that we must confess that we aren't perfect. We all have character flaws, quirks, and attitudes and beliefs that are in conflict with others'. By admitting we are different, we free ourselves of the pretense of being a good person all of the time.

Good people are well-adjusted, contributing members of society. Good people are not perfect people. They allow themselves to err and gracefully accept and apologize when they do make mistakes. Good people of different natures do indeed have conflicting values. It is the good people who take the time to be reflective and examine the nature of their being with a deep sigh of relief because they can admit to themselves and others that they are human. And to be human means to accept yourself in all your glory as well as in all your imperfection.

This might mean that you recognize yourself as a good professional and a good parent while accepting that you may have personal opportunities for growth with other relationships in your life. For example, some of us may have control issues, may have the desire to be a perfectionist, or may even have anger-management issues. Do you have the courage to admit to yourself that you're selfish, needy, or have irrational fears, control issues, or any other less-than-desirable character-istics or traits? I'm not suggesting we're all this way. However, most of us have some of these undesir-able characteristics to one degree or another. The point here is to acknowledge and accept our weaknesses just as we do our strengths, all the while working on accentuating the positives of our characters and working to manage or reduce the negative aspects through self-awareness.

The Importance of Self-Acceptance

Many of us are not willing or able to accept ourselves completely. We actually fail to acknowl-edge our faults to ourselves and others. Making oneself vulnerable is an act of courage. It takes courage to admit our shortcomings. We don't like to admit our faults for several reasons. One reason is that we fear being rejected, judged, or ostracized from a group. Another reason is that we want the approval and respect of others. We don't see oth-ers admitting faults, so why should we? We hold people in high esteem who seemingly have it all together. However, there is no such thing as hav-ing it all together, and upon a close examination of anyone, this fact will easily be confirmed.

So the question becomes: why? Why do I need to accept myself as I am? Self-acceptance is critical to our well-being. It is the basis of our self-esteem. Where do you get your esteem? Is it your work ethic? Is it your community service? Do you get it from being a good parent, sibling, or friend? Once we learn who we are and accept ourselves as we are, what others think of us becomes less important. The personal security I gain through self-acceptance enables me to be emotionally honest with myself and with others.

What would our world look like if we were all able to relax and just be ourselves all day long, regardless of whether we're at home or work? Even the small changes we make can have a positive and lasting impact on personal performance, team productivity, and our organization's success. Our culture is already evolving toward helping us do this. Do you recall the times when men wore suits and hats to baseball games? How about the early days of jet service when men and women alike dressed up to travel? Wearing ties at the workplace is virtually a thing of the past, except in a few professions like law and banking. Casual dress has become the norm, not only in the workplace, but for ball games and travel as well.

The days of dressing up and wearing suits for work have diminished because many people aren't comfortable being themselves when they're all dressed up. This is most evident when watching others who only dress up occasionally, like for a wedding, graduation, or funeral. It's almost comical to see the awkwardness of some people in these situations. It's easy to see that they just aren't themselves when they're required to dress in non-normal ways.

Fortunately, our culture is changing in many ways. For example, funerals used to be formal, solemn events characterized by a single eulogy. Today, many funerals are celebrations of the deceased's life, with many participants sharing stories and fond memories. These cultural changes are helping us to create situations in which we can act more normally rather than having to don a mask because we're uncertain how to behave.

Just as casual dress in the workplace assists us in being ourselves so we can be more productive, so too must we take off the masks that we wear to protect our egos. This is what we're discussing when we talk about removing the mask. When we remove the masks, we free ourselves to connect with others, thus enabling us to make more connections. And it is when I connect with others that I am at my best. The best of me comes out when mutual trust is developed with others. This trust occurs when we've accepted each other and ceased worrying about impressions or judgments.

Once we can be truly authentic with ourselves, we find that we need to moderate some behaviors, change others, recheck our attitudes and beliefs, and increase our tolerance levels for others who, like us, are genuinely authentic and wish others no harm. Much has been written about authenticity. Authenticity is being who you really are all of the time, not just when you're in your circle of close friends, out with the boys or girls, or with your significant other. Authenticity does not mean saying the first thought that comes into your head. Nor does it grant you a license to behave boorishly. On the contrary, authenticity requires a proper sense of self and tact. Gaining the self-understanding to become authentic requires deep personal reflection.

Using Self-Reflection to Unmask Ourselves

Personal reflection is a difficult task. It requires us to hold up a mirror to our personalities and characters. Mirrors accurately reflect who we physically are. For most of us, there isn't a day that goes by in which we choose not to look into the mirror. Imagine how uncomfortable we'd feel if we didn't primp and preen in front of the mirror each day. Now imagine how ugly we'd be if we didn't look in the mirror for any length of time.

Unfortunately, we don't have a mirror to look into to reflect personality and character. Herein lies the problem. We'd all like to think that we're getting good reflections when we take the time to examine our behaviors with others. We are not. Some of us will dissect confrontations at work with co-workers, friends, family, and significant others. And, as we have learned, these seemingly reflective conversations do not provide an accurate mirror for our behaviors.

When we share these stories of differences, we tell them in ways that encourage others to validate our feelings. Sometimes we embellish a little bit. Other times, we omit certain facts. Most of the time, we're seeking out someone who will side with us and make us feel better. Making someone feel better by validating him or her when we are only hearing one side of the story does not provide accurate feedback for the individual. Hence, the mirrors we surround ourselves with are again more like fun-house mirrors that make us look distorted in one way or another.

We even extend this psychological phe-nomenon of selective hearing to other aspects of our lives beyond our personality and character. If a person holds strong beliefs, whether religious, political, or moral, he or she tends to look for and validate information that supports those beliefs and to minimize or deselect information that con-flicts with those beliefs. Some of us even go so far as to use anecdotal evidence to support our positions. For example, it has been scientifically determined and accepted as fact that cigarette smoking is bad for one's health. Yet, ironically, I'll sometimes hear a smoker state something ridicu-lous like, "George Burns had a good cigar every day, and he lived to be over a hundred years old." We have an uncanny ability to be self-deceptive to protect our egos and perpetuate unhealthy behaviors even when we are flat-out wrong.

The Illusion of Accurate Feedback

The workplace is probably the single most toxic area in our lives. It is a place where virtually no accurate feedback is given. Forget the annual review process. It is probably the most dreaded event of the year for most of us. First, imagine yourself in any other relationship where you only give feedback once a year. Imagine having a conversation with your significant other that goes something like this, "Well, it's annual review time, honey, and I want to start by saying you generally had a good year. Back in June, you had to reschedule a missed dentist appointment. In July and August, you were late twice to our son's soccer games, and in May, you were a little slow on cleaning the garage and tending to the yard. As a result, I'd like to set up three good goals for us to work on this year. And finally, since you didn't score the highest in any of the categories I've judged you on, you'll get no raise in allowances for travel, entertainment, and clothing." Are you kidding me? Getting feedback only once a year? Tying the feedback to your financial well-being? And consider the fact that the feedback is generally one way. We don't get to give feedback to our supervisor. Talk about an uneven relationship.

Even if we could give feedback to our supervisors, it wouldn't be valid feedback for the primary reason of economic security. Who is going to tell it like it is to the boss when the boss has economic authority over him or her? With the risk of being terminated, being passed over for promotion, and putting a potential raise at stake, I assure you that any feedback would be well measured rather than truly authentic. Hence, we provide distorted reflections and very little possibility for accurate feedback for adjusting behavior.

In fact, getting accurate feedback is not possible in any relationship that is unequal in status. Examples of this include doctor/patient, teacher/student, supervisor/employee, and parent/child, and even relationships where two people are supposed to be equally yoked. Each of us has to recognize the fallacy of accurate feedback in these situations. Therefore, we must acknowledge this fact and learn how to counter it by becoming more authentic (that is, by taking off the masks we choose to wear). So if the people we surround ourselves with don't provide accurate reflections, and if the unequal relationships in our lives don't serve as a good forum for providing us with accurate feedback, what is the proper thing to do? Assuming that therapy and self-help books, like this one, can only provide glimpses of insights into ourselves, self-reflection is the only answer. The point here is that we need to be emotionally honest with ourselves before we can even think about becoming emotionally honest with others and building healthy relationships.

Equating Authenticity with Principled Living

Learning how to take off masks is akin to learning how to live a principled life. People who are duplicitous are wearing masks and are not living principled lives.

When we decide to live a more principled life, we are essentially learning how to take off the masks that are preventing us from being our authentic selves. What is a principled life, and why is it so worth living?

Principled lives are lived by people who have consciously framed out a way of thinking and being that serves them and the broader community in which they live. Try framing out a few principles for your life; it's difficult to do and even more so to maintain. You'll be surprised to see how quickly your own behaviors violate your principles. Let's take a simple one, for example: *honesty is the best policy*. If you suggest to me that you don't lie, then I must call you a liar. If you still maintain the claim that you've never lied, then you are denying your humanity. All children go through the process of determining right from wrong and truth from lies, mostly through experiential learning and from their parents. I don't care if it's a little white lie protecting the birthday boy from finding out about the surprise party you're planning or if it's a simple omission of facts like telling your wife that you just stopped off for a quick drink with your buddies when in reality you should have stated that you actually had three or four drinks and there were female friends there, too.

There are many schools of thought for living a principled life, including Christianity, Islam, Judaism, Taoism, Hinduism, Confucianism, and Scientology. Our parents, civic organizations to which we may belong, support groups, and educational institutions all provide frameworks for leading principled lives. My guess is that you may be somewhat aware of your principles. However, being somewhat aware and striving to live a principled life daily are two entirely different things. Most of us have got the big stuff down, like: *murder is wrong, stealing is bad*, and *cheating on your spouse is not a good thing*. Generally speaking, these are areas that we don't have to deal with on a daily basis.

It's the little stuff about our personalities that gets in the way of us leading principled lives. Wearing masks is what leads to our daily frustrations. The only ways to address any of these shortcomings are to use reflection and develop greater self-awareness. Self-awareness, by definition, cannot be taught. It requires you to sit in silence without stimulus. It requires spending some time alone each and every day—no television, no radio, no newspaper or Internet, no others, just you and your thoughts. Begin with reflection. Clarify your thoughts and governing principles; recognize quickly in which situations you wear masks, and begin to think about how to make small changes in your daily life to become more principled. Your approach and success in these endeavors will truly be individual and unique. It is difficult work. It is probably the most challenging work you'll ever do. Yet, as you begin to live a more principled life, you'll begin to see many positive changes in yourself and your relationships.

Part II:

Interpersonal Success Strategies

Chapter Four

IDENTIFYING AND OVERCOMING BARRIERS TO EFFECTIVE COMMUNICATION

Career-limiting behaviors stifle the possibility of advancement for many truly capable individuals. These behaviors are not as outlandish as one might expect. Rather, they are subtle behaviors we all practice but don't realize. While these behaviors occur on the individual level, the problem is compounded when two or more people *assume*, *cope*, and *pick and choose their battles*. These are three of the most career-limiting behaviors people exhibit. Learning about these three barriers and how to overcome them is vitally important to your success.

Assuming

Let's begin by examining the first of the three career-limiting behaviors: assuming. It is true we all have assumptions. Every time we meet people, we are quick to make assumptions, and we adjust our behaviors accordingly. Assumptions can serve you well in some cases. For example, if you correctly assume you are in a dangerous situation by processing your surroundings, you just may keep yourself out of harm's way. However, making assumptions about virtually every person you meet or every situation you encounter is certain to limit the potential quality of your interactions with others.

Assumptions guide our thinking and, therefore, our behaviors. Typically, from the moment we meet someone, we begin to assess who he or she is. Within the first minute of interaction, individuals have already begun to form first impressions of each other. First impressions, while often lasting, are many times inaccurate because they are based on very limited data. After these first impressions are made, we typically filter all future data about a person to reinforce that impression—ignoring information that is contrary. Often, when we meet someone new, we're guarded in our tone and tenor and are slow to reveal who we are. We are often so guarded in our behavior that we suddenly become conscious of what dictates proper behavior in the situation; thus we fail to relax and act normally. This is why we sometimes can't remember a person's name just after being introduced. We're too busy trying to make a good impression and, at the same time, trying to interpret the other person's first interactions that no true connection is made. We do this primarily to protect ourselves from interacting with others whose opinions and beliefs we don't know and which may very well differ from our own. We are careful to avoid discussing sensitive issues in an attempt to avert potential conflict. Politics, sex, and religion are just three examples of sensitive issues we avoid. While this is probably prudent behavior, these are not the type of situations and assumptions we're talking about here.

The assumptions I'm referring to here are much more subtle. These are the assumptions we make at work that start from the very moment we're first interviewed and last throughout the entire time of employment. Recall your first day on the job at a new organization. I'm certain you were processing myriad details from many sources and beginning to form opinions about your work, the job itself, your co-workers, your boss, the working conditions, moods, attitudes, and the like. If you're like most of us, you probably went home after work and had the requisite conversation about how the first day of your job went. You've probably already decided to some degree who's naughty and who's nice. You may have even decided who is a potential ally or confidante and who makes you feel especially guarded. You decided all of this on the first day of the job with very few real interactions and decidedly limited information.

While protective, these assumptions can be dangerous and career-limiting. Why is it that we can't suspend our judgments and take everyone at face value? Why do we feel as though we have to interpret the words and meanings of conversations? Why can't we just have open, honest dialogue? It's precisely because we choose to make assumptions rather than have clarity in our interactions with others. It is because we've been lied to, manipulated, and unwittingly taken advantage of at times in our lives, so we assume we have to be guarded with others to protect ourselves.

Reassessing My Reality

To gain this clarity, we simply need to learn the phrase that saves the day: "Can I reassess my reality?" *Reassessing my reality* is a wonderful expression of attitude that doesn't put the onus on others to rationalize their behaviors. Rather, using the concept of reassessing our reality puts the responsibility on ourselves rather than others.

For example, if someone makes a remark that startles you in some way, you may be inclined to adopt an offensive tone by saying something like, "Did I just hear you say that?" This statement clearly puts the other in an ego-defensive position. Instead, you can say something like, "Excuse me. May I check something out with you? I thought I heard you say this or that, and I just want to make sure that's what you meant. Did you mean to imply this by your statement, or am I just not hearing you correctly?" The latter attitude is one of curiosity and suggests that the offended one is possibly at fault for misinterpreting the statement or conversation.

It is best to avoid assumptions, gain clarity, and take personal responsibility for what you thought you heard rather than assume something negative about the other person. This is why *reassessing my reality* is the concept that saves the day. Learn how to use this concept, and you'll begin to see many of your conflicts with others and unintentional misunderstandings melt away.

Coping

Secondly, we develop coping strategies to deal with others in our organizations, thereby enabling unacceptable behavior. Again, we don't do this with a malice of forethought; we do this because we haven't developed successful strategies to overcome our fears or inability to deal well with others. We all have to deal with people in our lives who have some unacceptable behaviors. For example, we may have to deal with people who have quick tempers, who always have to have the last word, or who may not be respectful of others' contributions to the team. Thus, it becomes imperative to understand ourselves and decipher how others have developed coping strategies to deal with our undesirable traits, so we can address our own shortcomings.

Some people may be using coping strategies with you for a variety of reasons. Maybe you have a short fuse and are quick to anger. Maybe you're melodramatic. Maybe you micromanage people and have an condescending attitude toward your subordinates. Isn't it time you hold the mirror up and begin to hold yourself accountable for your unacceptable behaviors? Remember, though, that your task is not to hold the mirror up to others. It is only to hold it up to yourself. Perhaps an example can help illustrate this career-limiting behavior.

Do you find yourself doing *work-arounds*? A work-around is a coping strategy used by many people to avoid interacting with others. They work around a person, a department, or even a whole division within an organization. We work around someone or groups of people purposely. We do it to shield ourselves from interaction. It usually means that we're uncomfortable with someone or some possible unintended consequence. It happens when we have negative expectations about what will happen in the future if we take action rather than avoid a situation. These negative expectations are damaging because they aren't reality; they exist only in the minds of the fearful. When told to call someone about an issue, we may choose to send an e-mail instead. We may choose to go to that person's supervisor. We may choose to discuss it with human resources. Or we may even avoid the situation entirely. Here are some additional avoidance techniques. Which ones are you guilty of? Be honest and start checking them off.

✓ Timing a conversation for when you think a person is in a good mood

✓ E-mailing rather than responding directly in person

✓ Complimenting people to butter them up
✓ Feigning illness
✓ Telling white lies
✓ Denial or blaming others
✓ Agreeing with someone just to get out of the conversation

These coping strategies enable undesirable behaviors in others rather than help us get to the heart of the interpersonal conflicts.

Start today to begin the practice of identifying your top coping strategies. Confront them, and choose to act purposefully rather than succumb to your fears. Remember, too, that everyone else is using them as well, and therefore you're likely not having very meaningful or honest interactions with most of your co-workers.

Many people use the coping strategies listed above because of an imbalance of power in the relationship. They use them to level the playing field. The problem is that it doesn't really level the playing field. Instead, it just distorts the relationship further by enabling dysfunctional behavior on the part of both parties. Unfortunately, there is no such thing as a perfectly equal relationship. It just doesn't exist. When conflict arrives and push comes to shove, somebody gets to be the one to shove. Given this fact, we must realize that when we're on the lesser end of a power imbalance, we needn't seek to merely cope with it as our best alternative. There are better choices to be made.

One simple choice is to hold up the mirror when you catch yourself seeking to use a coping

strategy and begin an honest dialogue with yourself. Ask yourself what's preventing you from acting in a more purposeful way. By using a coping
strategy, you're actually exacerbating the situation. That is, you're making it worse by not confronting it and are therefore actually condoning
the behavior and enabling it to happen again in
the future. Instead of getting trapped into thinking about what might happen or developing
negative expectations or fears, think about what
it would be like to have authentic dialogue with
the other person and put the issue to rest rather
than waste precious energy that is better spent on
more positive aspects of life.

A colorful, time-worn joke illustrates the
concept nicely. A perfectly healthy, normal man
walks into a tailor to have a suit made. After going
through the ritual of being sized up and selecting
the fabric, the man waits and returns when the
suit is ready. Upon his return, he tries on the suit,
and it's a terrible fit. The right arm is way too long,
and the left leg is way too long. The man tenderly
objects to the fit. The tailor, not wanting to redo his
shoddy work, suggests to the man that he simply
needs to cinch up the right arm and hold the suit
down by cocking his head to the right and pinning
it into place with his chin. Similarly, the tailor goes
on to suggest that the man pull up his left pant
leg and hold it in place with his left fist. Unable
to cope with the thought and fears of further
confrontation, the man obliges, pays the tailor,
and walks down the street in his new suit. Shortly

thereafter, he is passed by two other men walking in the opposite direction. After passing the man awkwardly limping along, one man says to the other, "Poor fellow, what a terrible handicap he has." To which the other replies, "Yes, I know, but doesn't the suit fit well?"

Failing to assert yourself does indeed have its consequences. Some people call this failing to address the white elephant in the room. The reason they refer to it as an elephant is that the unstated conflict grew very large because no one had developed the skills to deal with the situation head-on before it became a bigger issue. They chose to develop coping strategies instead of being constructively confrontational. It is not the job of the human resources department to solve these problems, which exist in almost every working relationship. It is our job to become emotionally mature to the point of behaving constructively in our daily interactions.

This means that we address things in the present moment. It means we don't allow petty resentments to fester into larger interpersonal dysfunction. It means we keep our fears in check and stay in the present moment rather than spinning tales from negative fantasies. It means we listen to our inner selves and develop the courage to deal with the many little indiscretions that trouble us throughout the day. Let's not forget to pay attention to how others are coping with us, too. The signals are out there; we simply need to pay greater attention. Ask yourself what might be going on if you leave someone a voice message and you receive an e-mail back rather than a return phone call. Ask yourself what's going on if you can't enjoy a luncheon with all of your team members. Ask yourself what's going on if people give you nonverbal cues of discontent when you're speaking or leading a meeting. Please pay attention, as sometimes this is the only valid feedback you get, even though it's not directly expressed.

Picking and Choosing Our Battles

And finally, beyond assuming and developing coping strategies, we pick and choose which battles to fight and which to leave alone. We all do it. Picking and choosing which battles to fight actually compounds workplace tensions. This is due to fact that when one surrenders a fight, it creates resentment toward the other or others. Factor any number of people into the equation, and it's a wonder we are able to communicate authentically at all.

First, we must realize what it actually means to pick and choose different battles and how doing so undermines interpersonal effectiveness. When I say that I'm not going to fight a battle, the mere expression implies that there will be a fight and it will be a tough battle. Any person who approaches interpersonal conflict with the attitude of having to do battle does not have the skill set to work through the differences between two or more people. Oftentimes, when interpersonal conflict occurs, it's because there is an intersection of differences between the two people. Unfortunately, we don't have a system like a traffic signal that determines who has to yield and who gets the right-of-way in resolving interpersonal conflicts. It would be nice if we had a traffic signal system to deal with who has to yield and who gets the right-of-way when two people find themselves at an intersection of differences, but this is not the case. Therefore, it is up to us to figure out ways to resolve these differences.

Why do we pick and choose our battles? Most of us will respond that we don't have the energy to fight them all. And what zaps our energy? It is the fact that we have to juggle all of the emotions of dealing with unresolved conflict. It's really all about workplace politics. When two or more people gather together, there needs to be governance. Governance—or politics, per se—is simply the ground rules by which we interact. In every organization, there are ground rules. Some of them are written, while others are tacit. The culmination of these rules amounts to an organization's culture. Suffice it say for now that if we're not at the top of the organizational chart, we pretty much have to deal with the environment in which we're working. This is what causes us to pick and choose our battles. But it doesn't have to be this way.

While others you will be dealing with will still be practicing these undesirable behaviors, you must remember that if you change your behaviors, others, by default, will have to react differently to you. You must learn that picking and choosing battles is the wrong way to think about or approach the situation. Then you must recognize that conflicts left unresolved will only become greater with time and require even more of your energy to deal with. Knowing this is not enough to eliminate this undesirable behavior. To eliminate the barrier of picking and choosing your battles, you must begin to behave differently.

This is not intended to be a prescriptive book. I don't have the answers to your problems. I don't know how you're going to overcome these dysfunctions. The resolutions to these issues are uniquely individual. What works for me won't work necessarily work for you. What works for you won't work for me. Asking people for advice about what to do in any particular situation brings discussion, but ultimately, how the issue gets resolved is solely up to the individual with the issue. Learning how to resolve these issues for ourselves is the only way for us to liberate ourselves from codependence on others. It is the only way we grow. Asking others and taking their advice absolves us from taking responsibility for our own actions. If I take your advice and things don't work out well, I get to blame you. This is akin to looking out the window rather than into the mirror. Playing the blame game is detrimental to our personal development, and it is, in part, the subject of the next chapter.

Chapter Five

STOP PLAYING THE BLAME GAME
AND MAKE A PLAN FOR SUCCESS

An organization's culture determines which behaviors are appropriate. For example, charitable organizations, nightclubs, sports teams, government agencies, the military, and NASA all have distinct cultures that dictate which behaviors are appropriate to display and which are not. However, just as the culture of a country or society is constantly changing, an organization's culture is dynamic, too. It changes with new leaders, new team members, and new marketplace challenges, as well as myriad other factors.

The Blame Game

Although many cultures seem static and slow to change, they are all indeed dynamic. A look at the development of any organization over time will reveal different cultural periods. For example, the entrepreneurial characteristics of a start-up business will give way to a systems approach to doing business as the start-up matures and adds layers of management and bureaucracy. It is important to realize that because an organization's culture is dynamic, the appropriateness of any person's behavior is subject to interpretation over time. Barring the obvious (using vulgar language, stealing, etc.), most organizational cultures required behaviors are quite reasonable and logical from the individual person's point of view.

What's not obvious is the *why*, or the motive, behind the behaviors. Determining a person's motive or intent is virtually impossible. Thus, we can only react to what occurs. Without knowing why people behave the way they do, it becomes easy to make things up and play the blame game. If a person is storming around the office in a huff, all we really know is that the person is doing this. We don't know why. It could be anything from having just been disciplined to having had a fight with his or her spouse. Making up motives for others' actions is not reflective of a self-aware person. This is the fundamental reason we must avoid playing the blame game at all costs if we want or expect to be successful.

The problem with the blame game is that this behavior is counterproductive and ultimately destructive. It tears teams apart and serves no purpose other than to try to make others feel inferior by tearing them down with blame and inflating one's own ego with boasting and pride. When people behave in this manner, the answer to the question, "Why would anyone want to work with me?" is simple. We don't want to work with people like this. In fact, it is people like this who make our work lives miserable.

Now if we look at it from an objective viewpoint, that is, a viewpoint that's distanced from the emotions of the situation at hand, we find ourselves holding behaviors like this in contempt. Yet, because many of these behaviors are random, irrational, fear-based, and deliberate, they are difficult to manage and relate to. Supervisors and managers at all levels are not schooled in confronting these types of behaviors and are, therefore, woefully unprepared to offer constructive feedback. Consequently, a negative cycle begins around making assumptions, protecting our fragile egos, and making false statements about the motives of others. It doesn't take long for the negative cycle to spiral out of control. The net result is a workplace dogged by bickering, poor communication, and self-righteous indignation by individuals as well as teams and departments; this is essentially what I call the blame game.

To counteract this, we must first realize that we are playing the blame game. Further, we must recognize that *all* of us are subject to this phenomenon to one degree or another. Therefore, we are all to blame. Not one of us can stand innocently pointing fingers at others. The remedy for this situation is to stop focusing on others' behaviors and start focusing on our own. None of us wants to work with the perfect person. The perfect person doesn't exist anyway (except in the minds of the delusional). Thus, we are all subject to improving our own behaviors. Forget about why someone did this or that. Instead, focus on your reaction. You're likely to find that, more often than not, your reaction is just as irrational as the original seemingly odd behavior in question.

As an example, let's just take a simple team meeting scheduled for 1:00 p.m. Seven members are on the team. One is a no-show and someone remarks that it's because he or she probably didn't have the work done. Another shows up twenty minutes late, and someone remarks, "Another two-hour lunch, I guess?" The late person retorts, "Well, at least I make my sales goals." All the while, one team member chooses not to join in fighting these trivial battles, while another copes by checking e-mail and keeping quiet during the slow start. Finally, the newest team member blames the team leader for not being effective at leading meetings and wasting people's time. Thus, it should be clear at this point that blaming others is not only an unhealthy way of being; it absolves you from taking a closer look at your own destructive behaviors.

Making Conscious Choices

How we react to situations is an important indicator of who we really are. Since virtually everything is seemingly out of our control (except for how we react to situations), learning the discipline of making good choices regarding our reactions, attitudes, and behaviors is the only real thing we can work on to make ourselves better in terms of making people want to work with us and improving our own job satisfaction. In every situation we encounter, we have options. Our options always include our reactions, our attitudes, and our resulting behaviors. Most of us react out of primal instinct, which is self-preservation in distressing situations. This is similar to the *fight-or-flight* response mode we have whenever we feel cornered. Yet, we don't have to react unconsciously or without purpose. We don't have to react with our so-called animal instincts. We are potentially purposeful people. We have the ability to think and make choices.

The question becomes whether we will decide to consciously make our choices or react instinctively. Except in cases of imminent bodily harm to ourselves or loved ones, we have the time to react with consciousness, purpose, and conviction. And because we are afforded this luxury of conscious choices, we actually find that we are not totally out of control. We control the most important aspects of our lives: how we react in situations, how our attitude affects our state of happiness, and how our behaviors limit or liberate us from the shackles of our minds and emotions.

Becoming a person with whom others desire to work begins with making wise choices. Good choices begin with good information. Good information is objective. Objective information is not subject to opinion polls, especially polls of those around you. Objective information helps clarify our subjective feelings toward our choices. Objective information leads to better choices because it separates factual reality from subjective reasoning. Gathering such objective data is difficult. Many times, we're unable to get to the real facts of the situation, so our subsequent response also becomes a distortion of reality and may further compound existing problems.

We can't change our age, sex, health history, or many other variables. What we can change is our subjective reasoning toward these facts. We can subjectively reason our way into or out of anything we want. We often rationalize our less-desirable behaviors to others as if to suggest that there were outside forces beyond our control. Again, this absolves us from examining our behaviors rather than forcing us to learn how to make better conscious choices. To be sure, we all can probably recount a time when we raised an eyebrow toward someone's distorted rationalizations. We are no different. We have the same rationalizations from time to time ourselves. Yes, others look at us with raised eyebrows, but often we choose not to acknowledge that in order to serve our own purposes; essentially we dismiss the other person's reaction so we can remain feeling as though only our own perceptions of reality are important or valid. Others remain silent in their objections because their rationalizations are strong, and the resulting potential conflict isn't worth risking a breakdown in the relationship.

Holding Yourself Accountable

The problem with most adults is that we let ourselves off the hook. We rarely, if ever, choose tough love for ourselves. Instead, as self-governing adults in a free world, we continually modify our subjective realities to serve our needs at any given moment. Since there is no one watching over us to spank us when necessary, we sometimes end up making subpar choices for ourselves and have to rationalize the behavior if things don't go our way. Eventually, we learn to lament our situation, resign ourselves to a life in mediocrity, and become cynical about how much control we really do have over our lives, our happiness, and our future.

Now is the time to forgive yourself for the past. Now is the time to realize that you are in control of your choices and, to a large extent, in control of your future. Now is the time for you to reflect and figure out how to stop playing the blame game and begin taking full responsibility for your behaviors. Now is the time to craft a self-development plan that enables you to propel yourself, your relationships, and your career toward the success you always knew you could achieve.

Developing a self-development plan that actually makes sense is not a difficult chore. It starts with understanding the wheel of life. The purpose of the wheel of life is to illustrate the many aspects of your life that you are juggling. When you become aware of balancing your many competing interests, you begin to realize just how unconsciously you've been living. Let's take a fresh look at balancing the wheel of life.

The Wheel of Life

The wheel of life depicted above indicates the many areas of life that you need to keep in balance. While each of the areas is depicted in the picture as balanced, the reality is that you probably spend disproportional amounts of precious time in one or two areas and neglect others. When all elements are in balance (not in terms of equal time spent but in terms of focusing quality time in each area), you roll merrily along life's journey and are pleased with where you are going.

Notice the big empty space with a question mark. This area is reserved for life's little unknown surprises. It is said that life is what happens when you're making plans to live your life. Life includes stressors like illness, divorce, death, job loss, going back to school, and having children. These stressors have the potential to throw you out of whack or even cause a flat tire on the wheel of life, leaving you stalled in your tracks. When the wheel of life turns and your attention needs to be directed toward the top priority at the time (family, work, etc.), you may tend to rank other concerns as lower priorities. Notice that *self* is located at the bottom of the wheel. This is the person you often neglect most when stretched to serve others (significant other, children, work, etc.). When life throws in an unknown variable, you have the potential to get a flat tire or get stuck in a rut.

As a result, some aspects of your life may begin to be neglected. Many times, you don't even consciously choose which areas to neglect. Frequently, you begin to neglect the areas in which you have the greatest strength. If your family is particularly strong, you may choose to neglect it because you know that the ultimate strength of the family bonds will prevail. Marginal areas, like community involvement and volunteering, may tend to take a backseat. Regardless of which areas you neglect, you suffer. You suffer because you need all areas in your life to be rolling along for you not to get stuck in a rut. Often, you may find yourself stuck in a rut after spending long amounts of time in between one or two spokes of the wheel of life. It isn't until you have that "aha" moment that you suddenly realize you're neglecting an important area of life. That's when you have a flat tire and are no longer rolling along nicely. However, attending to the neglected area can often lead to unintentional neglect in other areas of your life. Thus, balance in the wheel of life becomes an important part of holding yourself accountable.

Making and Adjusting Your Plans for Life

Instead of letting this wheel of life spin out of control or get stuck in a rut, you need to consciously chart a course that includes nurturing all aspects of self. When the time comes for life to intervene in your best-laid plans with a giant question mark, you'd be much better off if you pulled out the wheel of life and made conscious choices with your partner, children, family, work, etc.

The following worksheet might serve as a nice example of how to make conscious choices that better serve your needs. As a starting point, list your current goal or an objective you're working on, and consciously (with your partner, family, children, etc.) choose your level of activities (acceptable to all concerned). When life interrupts the balance of your wheel with an unforeseen variable, modify your goals and consciously choose this modified plan to ensure the wheel of life keeps spinning. This constant rebalancing act has to occur when life throws unexpected events at you.

Current Goal or Objectives:	

Slice of Life:	Current Activities (time spent):	Modified Plan of Action:
Family		
Work		
Spirituality		
Self		
Community		
Friends		
(?) Complete as needed		

When we make conscious choices about how we want to live our lives and how much attention and devotion we want to allot to each and every aspect of our lives, including self, we become enablers of our own success. Making further course corrections as time passes, when we reach our goals, or when life intervenes again is an appropriate and meaningful way to make smarter choices and gain greater control over our lives.

This is your chief responsibility: to take care of yourself so you can be the best in the world for others. Keeping the wheel of life in balance during normal periods in your life enables you to make conscious choices regarding how you choose to live your life. And when the unforeseen arrives, it makes dealing with the life stressor a little bit easier.

Chapter Six

THOUGHTS ON THINKING, AUTHENTIC DIALOGUE, AND OVERCOMING FEARS OF FAILURE

In order to be held accountable for our thoughts, words, and deeds, we first need to understand how we think. Once we know how powerful our thoughts are and that they are the foundation of our words and deeds, we will begin to realize that we need to change the way we think. Albert Einstein is credited with saying, "The thinking that got us into this situation is certainly not the thinking that's going to get us out of it." Now, if I don't know how I think the way I think, how can I be expected to change the way I think? Here are some useful insights.

Thoughts on Thinking

First, let's consider some facts. Experts tell us that the average person is capable of speaking anywhere from one hundred fifty to three hundred words per minute. At three hundred words, that's about five words per second. Further, experts tell us that we're capable of thinking three to four times faster than the rate at which we speak. This puts our thinking at a rate anywhere from four hundred fifty to one thousand two hundred words per minute. That's a rate of over six thoughts to upwards of twenty thoughts per second. Whoa! I wasn't even aware that I was capable of thinking that fast. The synapses in our brains are firing so fast that accident victims often report things happening in slow motion because the brain is able to think it through so fast, yet the body is literally not capable of responding quickly enough.

One of the best ways of paying attention to your thoughts is retracing them to a mood change. Have you ever been sitting at a meeting and suddenly thought to yourself, *I'm bored?* Trace back through the immediately preceding thoughts that led to the thought of being bored. Here's a statement you might find interesting. Usually the thoughts are self-imposed and self-limiting. I'll bet some of your preceding thoughts were something like, *How long do I have to listen to this guy? He doesn't even know what he's talking about.* How about taking responsibility for yourself by saying, "I bore myself," rather than, "I'm bored." Now if you take responsibility for yourself by accepting the idea that it is indeed you who is boring yourself, you'll begin to behave differently. If you really don't think the person knows what he's talking about, why not respectfully interject a thoughtful critique or ask him for his willingness to entertain other points of view? Or, if you're truly courageous, you could simply ask to be excused from the meeting for personal reasons. And when someone asks for the personal reason, say you bore yourself and don't have the courage to take responsibility for your own actions by speaking up and adding value to the meeting.

Another way to change thought patterns is by doing what I call focused thinking. Focused thinking is purposeful in nature. Dedicate time to focus on improving an area in your life. Try it. It's very hard but very rewarding. Try a few of these on for size. How do I make my significant other feel more special in a truly new and meaningful way? What have I done differently this year, this month, week, or day to build my own self-esteem? Or, how can I begin to problem-solve an ongoing personal issue? Try focusing on one of those questions right now. If you're like most of us, you won't be able to stay on task for more than a few minutes. And you wonder why your life seems aimlessly adrift and somehow missing that something special. It's you; you're missing from your own life. Learn how to be your own best friend through focused thinking, and good things will happen.

Consider this focused thought exercise for a moment. It is our own tolerance for complacency that leads us to live lives destined for absolute mediocrity. The reality is that we don't need to live mediocre lives. We can all become much more than we are. We can have better relationships, better working conditions, and even greater purpose and meaning for our lives. Focus on what's working well in your life. Why is it working so well? What are the unique characteristics that make this area of your life special? Can they be duplicated in other areas of your life? Focusing your energies on what's working well and then trying to further promote these characteristics in other areas of your life is one of the single most beneficial ways to improve your life. Consider it as food for thought.

Self-Discipline

Your path to becoming a better person begins with a commitment to yourself. It's a commitment to self-development and a commitment that needn't be broadcast to others in an attempt to impress. Quietly begin to change in your resolve to make yourself better. Hold yourself accountable for your representations (what you say), your actions (what you do), and yourself (what you think). The idea of self-discipline as a path to personal joy and enlightenment is as old as the Eastern religions. Self-discipline begins with disciplined thought. This is what members of certain religions teach. They consciously choose to sit in silence learning how to control their thoughts. They take the time to reflect on and figure out which emotions lead to which thoughts and vice versa.

With commitment comes personal reward. By focusing on yourself and holding yourself accountable, you'll begin to reap intrinsic rewards. Intrinsic rewards are self-fulfilling; the reward is inherent in the work itself. Compared to extrinsic (or external) rewards—like recognition, bonuses, or additional time off—intrinsic rewards last a great deal longer because they embed within us true character.

As a marathon runner, I don't run 26.2 miles to get a coffee mug or T-shirt. I do it to prove to myself that I am indeed capable and am in excellent physical shape. Chasing extrinsic rewards is like a greyhound chasing a mechanical rabbit around a racetrack. The dogs never catch the rabbit because the track operator is charged with always keeping the rabbit just far enough ahead to keep the dogs working hard to win the race. What the dogs don't realize is that there is no real opportunity to catch the rabbit, and if they do, they're sadly disappointed that it was all an illusion. There was no real rabbit to catch and eat. It's time to start working on yourself in meaningful ways that pay off in long-term dividends. Standard by-products of this work include increased personal health, more meaningful relationships, and greater career success. The benefits of intrinsic rewards include higher self-esteem, among others, and a healthy self-esteem enables you to have greater authentic dialogue with yourself and others.

Authentic Dialogue

Authenticity is critical to success in every aspect of our lives. It begins (and ends) with learning the art of questioning. Yes, that's it. It's just that simple. However, mastering the art of sincere questioning and meaningful probing is not easy to do. We all know how to do it poorly—just make a flippant remark like, "Whose big idea was that?" To be sure, this is not what I'm advocating. What I'm advocating is improving yourself and your relationships though the art of questioning.

Think about the role of the psychotherapist. For those of us who have been in therapy, it is easy to recall; others will just have to imagine. The therapist is skilled and well versed in information about how the mind works and how it influences our emotions and our bodies. When you go into therapy, though, you are not lectured; you are asked questions like, "What happened? How did you respond? How did that make you feel?" Eventually, through the art of questioning, the therapist enables you to resolve your own problems. And the personal problems tend to stay resolved because you did the work yourself, through the therapist. When you leave therapy, you don't leave as knowledgeable as the therapist—you leave with your issues beginning to be resolved. My therapist is essentially just a good emotional and personal mirror to help me reflect on my thoughts and actions so I can become a better person.

Every day, you awaken, and before you leave the house after some ritual of preparing yourself for the day, the odds are that you look into a physical mirror. You do so to comb your hair, shave, brush your teeth, apply your makeup, or make sure your clothing looks good on you. We all know the importance of making these personal physical adjustments in order to be presentable to the public. Now, let me ask you, when do you look in the mental or emotional mirror? Most of us won't go a day without looking into a physical mirror, so why is it that we rarely choose to look into our mental or emotional mirrors? These mirrors are actually more important than the physical ones because what really makes a person ugly are his or her attitudes, prejudices, or certain characteristics of his or her personality. How often do you say, "Did I offend you or come off wrong?" or "Am I being too pushy on this situation?" Most of us don't ask those types of questions often enough. Now, some of you will assert that you look into these mirrors by talking with your friends. For many reasons, good friends don't always provide good reflections. Sometimes, they share the same faults as you; other times, they don't want to hurt your feelings so they minimize real feedback. This is because our friends usually aren't trained in providing feedback and getting paid to do it for a living; they're just plain no good at it. Consider, for example, what happens in a divorce. Neither party seeks out the opinions of the other's friends to ask for honest feedback. No way. They simply rally their own troops and get their own feelings validated (essentially just looking in a fun-house mirror) by playing the blame game.

So get your voice heard by asking sincere, probing questions, both of yourself and of others. You'll find that when you ask others for feedback, at first, they're likely to feel uncomfortable, unsure, or suspicious. After you practice it a while, you'll find that it's contagious. They will begin asking you questions about themselves. Couple that with seeking to understand them by asking good questions, and you won't ever have to pick and choose a battle again.

At work, you can learn to do this by adopting a penchant for curiosity. When a decision is handed down that you don't like, respond to it this way or in a similar fashion: "I understand that you've decided to cancel the project. I have a few questions. I hope you don't take them personally because they aren't intended that way. Can you help me understand your decision-making process on the matter? Did you realize the impact it was going to have on the team? Did you consider other alternatives? Is there any information I can provide that might make you change your mind? Will you tell me if you think I'm pushing back too hard because I'm really just trying to understand this decision, as it really affects me and my department?"

Since you are asking with sincerity and seeking to understand rather than to be understood, this authentic dialogue approach will help you to gain greater understanding and build better relationships. With this approach, one hopes, the decision maker will not feel threatened or become defensive. Chances are, he or she will probably thank you for your concern and support.

Sometimes—and this is important to remember—you are able to provide additional information that influences decision makers to change their minds or helps them make better decisions. This happens more often as you begin to master these practices and make them a habitual part of your conversations. You'll find that rather than debating behind closed doors, others will often come and ask you for your input because of your reputation of sincere questioning with attempts to gain greater understanding.

Authentic dialogue is simply speaking what you truly think or feel with discipline and tact. When telephone solicitors call and try to engage you in a conversation to secure a sale, they usually start by asking you a question with which you can agree. It's usually something like, "Good evening, Mr. Brown. How would you like an opportunity to save some money?" Now, what I'm really thinking is, *Who is this clown, and how can I get him off the phone?* In my case, it's easy because I usually just state that I'm not interested in participating in a sales call, thank them for their understanding, and hang up. However, some, if not most, of us answer the question because we're taught that it's not right to be rude by simply hanging up on people. So we end up engaged in a conversation that we'd really rather not be in, and our minds race on ever so fast to figure out how to get out of it in a comfortable way. Now, if we behave that way with a stranger—that is, finding ourselves in an uncomfortable position and yet unable to extricate ourselves in a tactful manner—imagine how potentially much more unauthentic we are with people we are forced to work with: our peers, subordinates, or bosses. Fears can be paralyzing, preventing us from true authentic dialogue in some of the most important relationships in our lives.

Overcoming Fears

The relationship we have with our superiors is unequal in nature and requires us to use tact when speaking authentically. This is because our bosses have economic authority over us, as they are able to determine our raises, our opportunities for promotions, and ultimately our job security. Being authentic with our bosses is like telling the emperor he's not wearing any clothes; it's very risky. Therefore, we often end up telling our bosses whatever we think they want to hear instead of telling them what we actually think or feel. When a bunch of direct reports tell their boss what they think he or she wants to hear rather than what they really think, is it any wonder the boss ends up making bad decisions? The value of authentic dialogue cannot be overstated. It does mean that we're going to have to learn to overcome some fears.

I completed my graduate and post-graduate work at the University of St. Thomas in Minneapolis, Minnesota. Painted on the ceiling of the main hall of the campus is a series of frescoes depicting the seven virtues; each virtue is wonderfully illustrated. The fresco for *prudence* is worthy of mention here. Prudence is wisdom. This is certainly a desirable characteristic most of us want. In this particular fresco, we see a woman who is adorned with cap and gown, having been dutifully prepared for success in life by the educating institution. In her left hand is the book of knowledge, and her right hand is raised as if she is taking an oath. She is standing before a columned Greek archway ready to walk into her future. Between her and the archway is a gigantic fire-breathing dragon with a scroll clutched in its right claw; its left claw is raised and poised to attack. The dragon is a mirrored image of the woman and twice her size. However, the dragon is not real. It exists only in the mind of the woman. Herein lies the lesson. The only thing preventing this woman's ultimate success in life is the dragon within her own mind. This fresco is important; it represents how we often fail to act in our own best interests because of our fears. Her own fears and her self-doubt about her ability to succeed are her worst enemies. To credit or blame anything other than ourselves for our own success, or lack thereof, is to choose to absolve ourselves of our chief responsibility to look into the mirror and hold ourselves accountable rather than looking out the window for something to blame.

Learning how to think in healthier ways, learning how to speak authentically, and overcoming your personal fears will undoubtedly lead to better relationships with self, in your personal life, and at work. This is the foundational work needed for you to become even more successful than you are today. Remember, how you learn to do it is up to you.

Part III:

Team and Organization Success Strategies

Chapter Seven

THE CULTURE CLUB—THE MEANING BEHIND YOUR ORGANIZATION'S DYSFUNCTION

Every organization has its own distinctive culture. Your organization's culture is deeply ingrained; it's not necessarily good or bad and is very often difficult to change. While most of us haven't formally studied organization culture, we're still highly aware and acutely attuned to its most subtle nuances. An organization's culture is powerful, and it is obvious to all who engage in the organization's activities.

Your organization has three distinct cultures. The first is formal culture; the second is the informal culture; and the third is the face of the organization to the public. Each of these three cultures is in constant tension with the other cultures. Showing you how to learn to understand and navigate the powerful forces of your organization's cultures is the objective of this chapter.

Your Organization's Formal Culture

Let's take a look at the formal culture of an organization. The formal culture is the culture established by its founders and leaders. This aspect of the overall culture is frequently captured in the lore of the organization's history and is usually taught to all new employees to provide them with a framework for understanding the origin, its founders, and their values and beliefs. For example, everyone who works for or volunteers with the American Red Cross is taught during orientation that Clara Barton was the founding mother. Similarly, people who work at Medtronic know that Earl Bakken was its founder. And, again, conventional wisdom has us knowing that Bill Gates is the founder of the personal computer industry. As time passes, the organization's history is often rewritten to make the stories of the founders seem larger than life. As the organization grows in stature, it becomes even more important to stress the founders' unique capability for foreseeing the value of the organization and its endless possibilities. Hence, the founders become larger-than-life figures themselves over time and inspire awe in the minds of the newly hired.

Along with the stories come the purported values and characteristics of the founders, who wanted them embedded throughout the organization. These values may or may not have been the driving principles of the founders, but somewhere along the way, they ultimately became attributed to them. Many organizations have institutionalized these values in the forms of mission, vision, and values statements. These are often carefully worded to make certain that every word captures a desirable trait and communicates said characteristics through the statement, and they are often prominently displayed, strategically, throughout the organization's hallowed walls.

The problem is that they often remain just that: prominently displayed, well-articulated wall statements. Do you know your organization's mission, vision, and values? Don't be too hard on yourself if you don't. Most of us haven't internally incorporated the formal cultural aspects of the organization by memorizing these statements. The main reason for this is simply that the formal culture is just that: formal. The formal culture is often in direct contrast with the informal culture of the organization.

Many times, while consulting with clients, I make this point by working with different levels of the organization and contrasting the differences after a simple exercise. I'm sure if you try this in your organization, you'll probably see similar results. The first part of the exercise is to ask everyone involved to individually write down the mission, vision, and values of the organization on the spot. To be sure, there are as many different answers as there are people submitting them. These different responses demonstrate a lack of organizational alignment, which will be discussed in chapter 9. After the exercise is complete, it becomes clear that the formal culture of the organization is really not deeply embedded within its leadership or its employees. When we recognize this, we can begin to see how organizational dysfunction emerges when everyone is seemingly on a different page.

The next step of the exercise is to separate the leadership of the organization from the rank-and-file members. In separate discussions with the groups, I pose these questions: "What does this organization stand for? And, what does it value?" The leadership team usually completes a very nice list of positive attributes and characteristics. It may include statements like, "We're all family here; we have an open-door policy; we value trust, honesty, and communication," and perhaps even one of the best espoused values ever coined in a phrase, "It doesn't matter if you make a mistake around here—it's how we deal with it that counts." Yeah, right! The rank-and-file members of the organization usually come back with a laundry list of items that frequently don't match those values espoused by the leadership. I get lists of values with characteristics like, "Productivity is number one; rank has its privileges; reduce errors; manage to the budget."

This begs the obvious question: which group is correct in its assessment of the organization's culture? The answer is *always* the rank and file. The rank and file is correct in its assessment, because they're the ones who have to work within the confines of budgets, compete for scarce resources, meet deadlines for bosses, etc. The senior leadership or executive team's perception is distorted. This is because they're stating the way that they *want* to see themselves viewed rather than how they actually *are*. They often want to be seen as caring, compassionate people, who balance the needs of the organization with the individual needs of the employees. This realization should be obvious to us all. After all, I want to be seen as wise, learned, caring, thoughtful, respectful, etc. But is this truly reflected in my everyday actions? The answer is yes only if the rank and file says so. It doesn't matter what I think about myself as an ambassador of the organization. What is important is how others are experiencing me. Their perception is reality when it comes to viewing leadership.

And so the formal culture of an organization has its basis in the stories of its origins. It is manifested in mission, vision, and values statements. It is espoused, albeit with varying degrees of clarity, by its senior leadership. It is often not aligned with how the employees view the organization. And the leaders, cognizant of this or not, are charged with changing it as needed to better serve all of the organization's stakeholders.

Your Organization's Informal Culture

Beyond the formal culture of an organization is the informal culture. The informal culture is quite different from the formal. The informal culture is dominated by *what* and *how* things get done and through *whom* these tasks are accomplished.

The informal culture is a function of everyone in the organization. It's how decisions get made. It determines whose voice gets heard. And it clearly identifies where the power in the organization is, regardless of rank or title.

Only through time can one truly learn the intricacies of the organization's informal culture. One usually has to attend many meetings to determine whose voice is getting the attention of the decision makers. A person usually has to go through a budget cycle or two to determine how scarce resources are actually allocated. Further, one usually has to discern which invisible boundaries not to cross through watching the trials and errors of oneself and others.

The informal organizational culture is just as important as, if not more than, the formal culture because it is a function of the organization's current workforce. It can change dramatically with the addition or subtraction of just one key individual. Sometimes, it can change with a switch in team leaders. Other times, it can change with the elimination of one toxic personality from the team. This fluid nature of the informal culture encourages power struggles within the organization.

The basis of power struggles lies in the political agendas of different people. Political agendas are used to wield influence and effect change. They are biased in nature and are detrimental to the organization's success. Any energy internally directed toward resolving internal conflicts is energy that is directed away from accomplishing the organization's mission; that is, it is wasted energy. Therefore, it is in the best interest of the organization to minimize these conflicts through creating awareness and facilitating the personal growth of its employees. This is the only meaningful way to minimize or cut out the politics within an organization.

We'll contrast the formal and informal cultures of an organization through an example. Let's use the concept that there are both formal and informal communication channels in an organization. This example will illustrate the power of the informal channels of communication. In this case, a memo is being distributed by a senior leadership team member inviting employees to an all-staff meeting to discuss declining sales revenue and relevant staffing levels. The memo is issued. The date and time are noted. Yet, before anyone attends the formal meeting, people are seeking information about the nature and scope of the meeting, primarily so they can determine how it may affect their organizational responsibilities or them as individuals.

The formal communication aspect of the organization's culture is the memo. The informal, though equally important, communication that ensues immediately is the reaction to the memo. The informal part of the organization becomes filled with rumors and speculation about the fallout from the meeting. People seek information anywhere they can find it. People will go to great lengths to determine if their futures are secure.

However, this information is not reliable. The reason for this is simple: when people don't know all of the facts, they tend to make up details to complete the story.

Yes, this is true. We guess, speculate, and arrive at our own conclusions by filling in all the data gaps with what we make up. Then we share our reality—based on our made-up data—with others to sift through and hopefully have it confirmed, regardless of whether or not it is accurate. An example of this is what happens in an office when a member of the team is terminated. If the organization is practicing sound human resources principles, the reasons for the termination should be guarded as confidential. This is true unless the circumstances surrounding the termination would inadvertently hurt the organization if not properly addressed to the group as a whole. However, people still want to know the reasons for the termination, and they quickly take what little factual data they have and make up the rest of the story to provide some logical continuity to what just occurred; that's just human nature.

This part of the informal culture, coupled with additional negative aspects, is the source of many employee frustrations and must be addressed. We all know what these other negative aspects are and probably experience them on a daily basis, like with the person who kisses up to the boss, the person who fudges the numbers a little, the person who abuses the personal time-off policy, and so on.

All of the situations described are, for the most part, not under the control of the average employee. Leadership must address these issues. In my experience, most of the organization's leadership lacks the fundamental skills and abilities to deal with these situations effectively. This is due primarily to their lack of training in leadership. That's when it starts to blow up into a much larger issue. Sadly, this justifies the need for human resources to intervene in direct-line authority issues. Had the leaders developed the skills to deal with these aspects of management, these problems wouldn't exist or, at the very least, would be minimized.

It is the intersection of the formal and informal cultures that creates tension in the organization. Employees are frequently not empowered to effect change. Sadly, they see these dysfunctions daily, hope for good leadership intervention, and, without any, resign themselves to the situation, making statements like, "That's just the way it is around here; it's just our culture," or they simply resign.

Your Organization's Public Face

Crisis management is an important aspect of any organization. The face of the organization is usually represented by a spokesperson who has the authority to issue press releases and speak with the media. What is important is that the integrity of the brand is maintained throughout the crisis; therefore, the cultural face of the organization must be in place long before any potential crisis arises. This is the cultural face of the organization to the community; this is the brand, per se. Ideally, it should be well aligned with the other cultures in the organization.

Hence, we see the need for a cultural face of the organization to present to the community. The realists among us relate this to the public affairs department or the investor relations department. The cynics among us call it the spin room—you know, the place where leaders huddle together when a crisis occurs to figure out how to spin the issues in a positive light. There is truly a need for a cultural face to an organization, but if it is not in close alignment with the formal and informal aspects of the organization's culture, it creates tension and won't pass the scrutiny of the public eye.

The face of the organization, like the other cultural aspects, is very difficult to change. It needs to be proactively managed, as it is essentially the reputation of the organization. Huge amounts of energy and money must be spent to develop and maintain the face of the organization. Once an organization's reputation is established, whether good or bad, it lingers in the marketplace for a very long time. Just as with individuals, reputations, once established, are hard to shake. Further, marketing gurus tell us that it takes incredible amounts of money to regain the loyalty of lost customers. It is clearly better to maintain the bonds of trust through the face of the organization than to try to regain them.

When any of the three aspects of the composite organization's culture are out of alignment, it creates tension. Therefore, it is important to actively manage all three cultural aspects. I find that, many times, organizations' leaders do this only as a reactionary measure when the need arises. However, the organizations whose leadership takes the time to proactively manage these sociological concerns are the ones that gain the competitive advantages in the marketplace. The importance of cultural congruence cannot be overstated here. There are no prescriptive solutions. Each organization must figure out these answers for itself.

Chapter Eight

VIRTUAL TEAMING OR VIRTUALLY TEEMING— THE SUBTLETIES OF MEETING SUCCESS

In today's high-tech, digitally oriented world, nearly everyone performs some capacity of his or her job in a virtual environment. Whether it's checking e-mail at home or off-site, conference calls, or video conferencing, virtual teaming is here to stay. In my experience, this leads many of us to be virtually teeming with frustrations about how our time is best spent. Nowhere does this occur more often than in the countless meetings we attend, regardless of their type.

Meeting Basics

Too many meetings, meetings, meetings! This is perhaps the number-one lamentation I hear from people when asked about their likes and dislikes at work. When will they ever end? Not anytime soon in today's fast-paced world. Meetings are a necessary evil. They do serve an important function in ensuring the organization's success.

Nearly every person I speak with about the positive and negative aspects of his or her job has negative impressions on how meetings work (or, actually, fail to work).

The complaints, while varying in some cases, center around several key aspects of meeting management: frequency, duration, composition, lack of consensus, and the lack of leadership designed to make them truly effective. However, you probably don't have the power to single-handedly change many of these aspects of the meetings you're required to attend. Thus, it's in your best interests to learn a few basics of meeting management to help limit your frustrations and make the most out of meeting times.

Many of your organization's meetings are probably unnecessary: weekly reports, monthly and quarterly updates, standing committees, and the countless operational and planning committee meetings. If the frequency of the meetings seems too great, how does an organization learn to do more with less when it comes to meetings? First, we need to ask if the frequency is too much or just right. An easy way to answer this question is to ask yourself if the amount of meetings you attend affects your ability to satisfy all of your other job responsibilities. A good strategy is to make a list of all of the meetings you attend in a given period, the length of time you spend preparing for the meeting, and the duration of the meetings, and then compare that total with the total work hours for the period. Simple division will yield the percentage of time you spend in meetings. I'll bet you'll be surprised at how much time you spend in meetings relative to your total workload. When feasible, seek out your co-workers and boss and try to reduce your physical meeting times. All will be pleasantly surprised how many meetings can be conducted through other forms of communication.

Meetings are generally unnecessary if they are simply used to update others on the status of where you are with your projects. Update meetings should only be required when one aspect of the team has been identified as underperforming and the team needs to recalibrate or make course corrections. Information exchange for team-member updates should be done electronically. Opponents of this strategy will suggest that face time is really necessary. Telephone conversations work really well for most issues, with the exception of managing conflict, which requires having a crucial conversation in person.

Crucial conversations do require face-to-face interaction in order to ensure the highest probability of success. Because of the high stakes, these meetings are necessary, as they require the participants to do more than just listen to words. Many of us have been taught that nonverbal cues make up a large percentage of the communication process. When issues of credibility or integrity arise, it is important to be able to read all of the cues in the communication process. A simple blush, pursing of the lips, sitting on one's hands, and a roll of the eyes are just a few examples of nonverbal cues that can be the telltale signs of the conversation's true meaning.

Meeting Lengths

The duration of meetings is frequently an issue. They often either run long or are arbitrarily cut short of completing business because of a time limit. Neither option is desirable. The length of the meeting should always be minimized if possible. Remember the old adage that work always fills up to the time and space allotted. Longer meetings invite orations, multiple-point counterpoints, and general malaise for those whose voices are not heard. Sometimes leaders will want every department head to give a five-minute update in a meeting. No real comprehensive department update can be delivered in five minutes, and after the first several updates go too lengthy with discussion, other updates are abandoned as the meeting agenda gets modified midstream to meet the time deadline. I like to use the technique of stating that department updates must contain only two PowerPoint slides and the font must be sized at twenty to twenty-four points to limit the data. People who are frustrated by this limitation need to learn how to capture the message of their concepts in more succinct ways.

Another issue with meeting duration is the inverse correlation between the length of meeting time and the amount of time selling the meeting decisions to affected constituents. That is, if a team discusses a complex issue like compensation or next year's health plan for six or more hours, it's because it was a complex issue with many variables to consider. When the team members in the meeting go to debrief their respective reports, the same questions addressed in the meeting will arise in the ensuing discussions; this requires selling the reasons the committee made the decisions they did. This is best accomplished by having the most credible team members representing their constituents.

Intact Teams Versus Interdisciplinary Team Meetings

Meetings are often held by groups of intact teams like marketing, finance, human resources, operations, administration, and executive. These intact teams in meetings are potentially marginalizing the organization because they do not contain input from other parts of the organization that will be affected by the decisions made in the meetings. Conclusions are arrived at only to be vetoed by another department head, because the intact team failed to consider the ramifications for each and every other department. Further, since the intact team members are all of like mind (marketers are supposed to be creative; finance people ought to be risk averse and linear in thought; etc.), the resulting decisions from intact team meetings are often not optimal because the decision-making body is not made up of a cross-functional team.

The proper composition of meeting members should always hold fast to the rule of inviting others with a vested interest in the outcome. For example, the next year's health-care meeting should include (if not at least one or two other department heads) a member or two from the employee rank and file to witness the complexities of the decision-making process. Make sure the voices of these employees are heard, and then they, in turn, can serve as stewards to fellow employees. Messages from peers involved in the process are virtually always better received than messages from higher-ups since some may have contempt for having to live by decisions without having their voices heard.

Planning or Taking Action—Yes

An additional meeting composition consideration is allowing members with varying propensities for meeting tolerances to participate on different levels. For example, action-oriented people don't tend to like three-hour planning meetings, yet their place on the meeting team is still required. In these cases, do your best to frame out the issues and release the action-oriented people at various times throughout the meeting so they can begin the work being assigned to them. The planners of the group, who like meetings, as evidenced by acts like jumping up to the flip chart to begin making lists, should be taken advantage of and made to be the scribes or leaders of the process. Realizing the different roles people play and taking advantage of their natural differences will bring fluidness to meetings that team members will like. After all, there is nothing worse than the feeling of being held hostage at a meeting.

Standard group dynamics suggest no more than six to eight for the ideal team size in meetings. My experience suggests that when the team gets beyond that size, the dynamics change. A meeting with ten people is usually dominated by two people, interspersed with four other attendees, with the remaining team members either multitasking, daydreaming, or following along loosely in case they are called upon to make a contribution. When that happens, the latter often respond to a question with, "I'm sorry, could you please say that again? I didn't quite get it." The properly sized group yields optimum results. Conversely, having too few team members limits the creativity and effectiveness of the team.

Voting and Consensus

One final consideration for team size is whether the team is going to deal with a contentious issue that will require voting. Regardless of whether the team is task-oriented or not, voting groups should always contain an odd number of people. The odd number of people ensures no deadlocks. Bear in mind that one vote means one vote. Sometimes, because teams are composed of members with different ranks within the organization, junior team members may in essence proxy their votes to senior members because of some irrational fears. If you suspect this may be the case in your organization, you can guard against this by using a private balloting system. While not an ideal substitute for authentic dialogue or a level playing field, it does help the process if your organization hasn't effectively dealt with these best practices.

Gaining consensus in team meetings is difficult. While consensus may be desired, it rarely occurs. This is when the "meeting after the meeting" takes place after agreement and adjournment. I can't tell you how many times I have seen a decision made in consensus, and immediately after the meeting, people leave in pairs, threes, or fours to vent to each other, say what they really wanted to say in the meeting, and voice concern. The meetings after the meetings have to stop. If you experience this phenomenon in your organization, it is a sure sign that there are trust, communication, and authenticity issues. In my experience, I've found that it's best to go on the record during the meeting, state your views and objections, agree to disagree, and support the decision of the larger group when the meeting is over. At least you'll leave knowing that your voice was heard as a member on the minority side of that decision.

Detailed or Broad Agendas

Meetings, like many other aspects of the organization, need true leadership to keep them functional and productive. The myriad facets that can go wrong often do, not with intent, but due to a true lack of understanding on how to run meetings well. First, agendas with detailed time frames need to be tossed out—Five minutes for opening remarks, ten minutes for introductions, thirty minutes to frame the issue followed by a one-hour discussion and a fifteen-minute break. These types of agendas are usually off the mark after the first five minutes of the meeting. I find it better just to list the block of time and the requisite steps. In this case, I'd list a one-and-a-half-hour meeting time with the four tasks that need to get accomplished: opening remarks, introductions, framing the issue, and open discussion. This relieves the pressure to stick to the time schedule, which can force energetic discussions to an untimely close in order to move on to the next agenda item.

It is always a good idea to omit scheduled breaks as well. Morning meetings from 8:00 a.m. to 12:00 p.m. usually have a break scheduled in at mid-morning. I've found that because of the many liquids people drink at the start of the day, a break is usually well received just about forty-five minutes into the meeting. It's just a natural time for people to use the restrooms. Making participants sit when they are uncomfortable will probably have adverse effects on individual participation as attentions get distracted. In addition, scheduled breaks do not follow the true ebb and flow of the meetings. Discussion is squelched just prior to break time in order to get an arbitrarily timed break in. All meetings have a natural flow in terms of energy and participation. It is the wise leader (or facilitator) who recognizes the flow of energy and participation and pauses for breaks at their natural time of occurrence rather than scheduling breaks. Frequently, this is between major topics.

Ditch the Ground Rules

Additionally, ground rules for meetings don't add value. Why would we have any different behavioral expectations for meetings than we would for any other aspect of human interaction with the organization? If we do this, we're actually encouraging different standards of behavior depending upon what context you're in at the organization. Ground rules for acceptable behaviors need to be established during the hiring and orientation process, not for different committees or situations. Some people use ground rules so they have something to fall back on should an inappropriate behavior arise. This is just a safety net for people who don't have the skills to deal with special situations on a case-by-case basis. So save the precious meeting time for actual work rather than agreeing on new arbitrary principles that apply only in the meeting setting.

To keep your teams from virtually teeming with anger and resentments, it behooves you to learn the basics of meeting principles. When properly applied, they will help make your meetings more effective, efficient, and fun. As you learn to implement these best practices, you'll begin to see rises in both meeting productivity and employee morale.

Chapter Nine

THREE SIMPLE SOLUTIONS--PEOPLE, ALIGNMENT, AND SERVICE

Having the right people, aligning them to work well together, and embracing an attitude of serving others as fundamental aspects of leadership are critical steps to ensuring the highest probability of achieving your organization's goals and objectives. Each of these concepts will be illustrated via a story in this chapter. Further, this chapter will empower readers to understand that these concepts serve as a launch pad to put people first, get everyone aligned on the same side of the tug-of-war, and seriously curb autocratic management styles.

People—Your Organization's Single Greatest Asset

If "location, location, location" are accepted as the three greatest keys for selling real estate, then "people, people, people" must be accepted as the three greatest keys for ensuring your organization's success. Let's start by taking a look at two large, well-known retailers: Target Corporation and Kmart. While seemingly very similar in nature, these two retailers are vastly different. One is thriving while the other is barely surviving. Target is working diligently to open more stores and compete even more vigorously with the nation's biggest retailer: Walmart. Kmart, on the other hand (as of this writing), is being operated under the protection of bankruptcy court and is seeking a successful reorganization.

First, let's look at the similarities between Target and Kmart. They both sell commodities and sundries. Walk into either of the stores, and you'll see very similar product lines. Hygiene items, pharmaceuticals, small electronics and home furnishings, clothes, and the like are sold at both stores and at competitive prices. But that is where the similarities end and the differences begin.

To contrast these two giant retailers, we must look at some obvious differences. Foremost is store location. Target likes upscale suburbs while Kmart chooses to locate its stores in less affluent neighborhoods. Target has fewer stock-keeping units (SKUs), enabling it to merchandise its products with greater room for shoppers, or guests, as they like to call them. Kmart offers more SKUs, but it costs in the merchandising area, as its aisles are narrower and more densely packed. Target keeps an extra person or two up front at the cash registers at all times to ensure its guests don't have to wait long to check out. Kmart seems always to have long lines. Target stores are pristine. Even in the Northern climates where snow and slush can present cleanliness challenges, the Target stores remain clean. Kmart, on the other hand, doesn't seem to make cleanliness as high a priority. There is also a difference in the quality of some goods, especially clothing, where Target again seems to have a competitive advantage. Yet, none of these physical, easily defined differences speak to the real difference between the organizations: the people.

The people Target and Kmart choose to employ is the only real difference between the organizations. Stores don't decide where to locate themselves—people select locations. The number of SKUs is a function of people in supply-side management. Having extra staff on and keeping a watchful eye on cleanliness is again a function of management making decisions. So I posit that the only significant difference between the two organizations is their leadership. If we were to switch the leadership teams of Target and Kmart, it wouldn't be long before the organizations transformed into each other. That is, Target's leadership team at the helm of Kmart would make it a thriving organization, and conversely, Kmart's leadership team, with its decision-making mind-set, would turn Target into an entity that would barely be surviving.

The question then becomes what is it about the people that makes the difference between the organizations? It is their ability to make decisions more effectively, their ability to work together more effectively, and their ability to maximize individual effectiveness. Hence, it's the personal, interpersonal, and organizational effectiveness that sets them apart. How individuals, teams, and organizations do this is unique and up to each entity. However, the insights and ideas proffered herein, if heeded, will help take you, your team, and your organization to greater successes.

I find it odd, though, that most people don't seem to grasp this simple concept. It is indeed the people who make or break an organization. The next time you compare or contrast organizations competing for your business, realize that the only single variable making a difference is the decisions made by the people within the organization. If an organization attracts you because of its high standards, I guarantee you the people at the top have high standards. If an organization is offensive to you in some way, be certain to know that someone within the organization is allowing that. Simply put: it's the people!

Aligning Your Leadership Team

Alignment is the second of the three critical factors. Alignment is having everyone on the team know the organization's goals, its strategies and tactics, their role on the team, and how failing to perform, even briefly, may seriously impact achieving these goals. Imagine for a moment that you're part of a senior leadership team that is charged with the success of the organization. This is the group of people who have the decision-making authority and ability to allocate resources throughout the organization. The executive branch is present (CEO, CFO, etc.); marketing, human resources, operations, and logistics are all present in the meeting as well. Without being allowed to speak to each other, they are each tasked with writing down the organization's goal, its strategies and tactics, their own and every other team member's role in meeting these objectives, and how individual failings diminish the probability of the organization's success. Sadly, I've done this exercise many times, and the written answers of the senior members of the team are not only out of alignment but also sometimes vastly different characterizations of the same organization.

Now let's take a look at a professional football team. Imagine for a moment that you're on the sidelines of a football game on a Sunday afternoon. Every person standing on one side of the sidelines is on the same team. Pretend as though you don't know the game, its objective, how it's played, or even how it's won for that matter. If you tap any person on that team and ask him the goal of the game, he will say that it's to win the game.

"How?" you may ask.

"Score more points than the other team."

"How do you do that?"

"Well, we have three strategies: offense, defense, and special teams."

"And how do they work?"

"That's the tactics part of it. The offense has a playbook of optional ways to move the football forward and score. Similarly, the defense has a similar playbook to prevent the opposing team from doing just that. The special teams work in similar ways, albeit to a much lesser extent than the offense or defense."

"And what's your role?" you may ask.

Regardless of the role the player is assigned, he knows his role and how it affects the team. The player may be a quarterback, wide receiver, lineman, linebacker, or even the placekicker for the team. To a person, each knows his role, responsibilities, and the consequences of failing to perform. The team may play very well together for the entire game, but if the placekicker misses the winning field goal as time expires, the game is lost.

The point here is that the most well-aligned and interdependent team is the team that will excel and consistently beat the competition. Multiple agendas, putting personal interests ahead of the team, and not being personally and professionally well aligned are sure symptoms of an underperforming organization. Acknowledging the value of having the proper people on the team, coupled with aligning them well, is a strategic imperative for successful organizations.

Inverting the Management Pyramid

Finally, we turn our attention to service and the concept of leaders learning how to serve the people of the organization rather than being served by them. Most organizations have organizational charts depicting the hierarchy and titles of everyone. The higher the rank, the higher the position on the chart, and presumably the greater potential impact the individual may have on the success of the organization. Unfortunately, the higher positions of authority bring with them many perks, including lofty titles like chief executive officer (my favorite is one the military uses: supreme allied commander—now there's a title to be proud of), higher rates of pay, expense accounts, and first-class flights. It is specifically these perks associated with high-ranking corporate officials that seduce them into thinking that the organization is there to serve them. These managers then adopt the attitude of being indispensable, believing the myth of the hero leader, and are often quite demanding of and insensitive to subordinates, especially if performance is suffering somewhere under the purview of the direct report. This type of attitude by executives and senior leadership is caustic to the organization.

These attitudes do not serve the needs of the organization well. Instead, they bring fear, politics, intimidation, and ultimately dysfunction to the very organization whose success they are charged with ensuring. Let's say there's a logistics problem causing a shortage of product, demand is pent up in the marketplace, and sales are flat or suffering as a result. The norm for leaders is to gather the top members of the leadership team and ask for answers. What went wrong? Where's the problem? Who's responsible?

These questions invite mistrust, misinformation, and blame. They do so because they imply consequences for failing to perform. When a person feels threatened by having to defend a mistake, the result is frequently a skewed account of what happened, especially if the error was caused by neglect or a simple omission. Now I am not advocating tolerating poor performance or eliminating consequences. I am simply transferring the onus of the problem onto the leader, who is demanding answers. I am merely suggesting that the problem is that of the highest-level leader in the organization.

But how can that be? It is the leader's responsibility to ensure that every employee has the necessary materials, resources, and processes to successfully do his or her job. In essence, the leaders must adopt an attitude of taking responsibility and asking themselves, "How did I fail the organization? What details did I overlook? What did I fail to anticipate? Why didn't I monitor the situation more closely? How did I fail to communicate the importance or urgency of the problem?" The leaders need to invert the organizational pyramid and further ask to their direct reports in an attitude of service: "What can I do to help you achieve your (work) goals? What obstacles can I remove from your path to enable your (our) success?"

This is an attitude of ownership—not blaming, not demanding answers, not threatening consequences, but taking full responsibility for all actions under the realm of control. Other societies embrace this to a much larger degree. When a Japanese short-haul Boeing 747 crashed, killing more than five hundred people, making it the worst aviation disaster in Japanese history, the director of maintenance, once he determined that the crash was due to a mechanical malfunction that one of his team members was responsible for, did the only honorable thing a person could do in his society: he committed suicide. Yes, the director of maintenance took his own life. He blamed no one. He understood that the people flying his airline trusted him to do his job correctly and thereby ensure the safety of the passengers. When he realized he had failed, the only option for him was clear: take ultimate responsibility.

Not only do our leaders fail to take responsibility, they fail to serve the very organizations they were hired to protect, nurture, and grow. This is the bottom line: we have to hold ourselves accountable. We have to look into the mirror and take ultimate responsibility for each and every action we take. This is our chief responsibility.

www.ingramcontent.com/pod-product-compliance
Lightning Source LLC
Chambersburg PA
CBHW051541170526
45165CB00002B/825